A MANAGER'S GUIDE TO
ELDER CARE AND WORK

A MANAGER'S GUIDE TO ELDER CARE AND WORK

John Paul Marosy

Foreword by Bradley K. Googins

Quorum Books
Westport, Connecticut • London

Library of Congress Cataloging-in-Publication Data

Marosy, John Paul, 1951–
    A manager's guide to elder care and work / John Paul Marosy ;
foreword by Bradley K. Googins.
       p.   cm.
    Includes bibliographical references and index.
    ISBN 1–56720–229–2 (alk. paper)
    1. Employer-supported elder care assistance—United States.
I. Title.
HF5549.5.E34M37   1998
658.3'82—dc21   98–6022

British Library Cataloguing in Publication Data is available.

Library of Congress Catalog Card Number: 98–6022
ISBN: 1–56720–229–2

First published in 1998

Quorum Books, 88 Post Road West, Westport, CT 06881
An imprint of Greenwood Publishing Group, Inc.

Printed in the United States of America

The paper used in this book complies with the
Permanent Paper Standard issued by the National
Information Standards Organization (Z39.48–1984).

10 9 8 7 6 5 4 3 2 1

To my parents
Michael G. "Jack" and Agnes Marosy
in loving memory

Contents

Illustrations

FIGURES

TABLES

Foreword

Bradley K. Googins

Walk into almost any corporation today, head for the cafeteria, and sit with a group of employees, and you will find a universal conversation around the challenges of parenting, maximizing scarce periods of time, and trying to find balance between work and family. In an increasingly complex web of work and home demands, most employees have found little guidance from previous generations in successfully finding ways by which these demands can be met and incorporated into a model of healthy work/life.

To take but one example, it was only a generation ago that issues of raising children were neatly delegated to the home and family primarily through the role of the stay-at-home wife. However, a changing social and economic environment has not only brought these caretakers into the work place but has upset the conventional roles and responsibilities of homes and work places. The most basic set of parental responsibilities of families have now become reconfigured through a series of changing demographics and social values. Work places now find themselves the locus from which most adults are attempting to manage child care and elder care responsibilities. Since community resources have not been created to recognize and respond to these changes, an even greater source of stress has been created, as working parents and employees with elder care responsibilities have to go it alone, trying to meet the demands of the work place and their desire to carry out their dependent care roles and responsibilities.

The creation of the family-friendly corporation is a recent response that recognizes the uncomfortable bind that many employees find themselves in trying to be committed and productive employees while also trying to meet the needs of their families. In the early stages of family-friendly corporations, the issue of child care quickly arose to the top of the agenda. The entrance of young mothers with children has been the most visible manifestation of these new work/life dynamics and has resulted in the broad array of resources and referral services in on-site, back-up, and ill-child care centers, along with new organizational structural responses such as job sharing, telecommuting, and flexible schedules. While this focus on children is understandable and immediate, there also exists another series of dependent care needs brought into the work place by employees: the care of elders. By most measures, the growing demographics of our aging population will dwarf the current focus on children, and will constitute the most dominant dependent care issue as we move into the twenty-first century. In fact, most corporate work life programs are now discovering the issue of elder care and the need to respond to those issues.

It is important to understand that the issue of corporate elder care is by most measures more complex than that of child care and considerably more challenging to the corporation in terms of how to respond to employees with these issues. Child care is bounded by a discrete number of years, after which public institutions such as schools take over. Child care is also responsive to a wide range of formal and informal services that offer a range of options to most working parents. In contrast, elder care can be complicated by distance in which parents and working children are often living considerably far apart. In addition, elder care is a health issue, which is unpredictable in its course and can continue for many years.

Since most employees are pushed to the limit in trying to creatively meet the often conflicting demands, it is no wonder that levels of employee stress are at an all-time high. Consequently, the work place of today is significantly challenged by an issue such as elder care and is actively searching for models by which employers and their supervisors can find ways to minimize the tension and stress of caregiving while creating organizational responses that meet the needs of a productive work place with the caregiving needs of the employee.

A Manager's Guide to Elder Care and Work is a book that is sorely needed by both employees and work places. Caring for elder relatives will become an even more common place occurrence as the graying of the population continues, and as the baby boom reaches retirement age. It becomes critical that work places understand this phenomenon and begin to create supportive resources for their employees. In particular, supervisors and managers at all levels are confronted with employees facing elder care dilemmas. Situations that arise requiring employee time and commitment for an elder relative will often spill over into work demands, creating new challenges for the contemporary manager. Since the situation of managing working caregivers is relatively new to America's work force, little information is available and few guidelines have been developed that can assist managers in this delicate and often emotionally draining situation. John Paul Marosy's comprehensive guide provides both the information and guidelines by which supervisors can begin to sort through and manage what are often complicated and time-consuming situations.

Getting this book into the hands of America's work places, both working caregivers and managers, will go a long way towards building a foundation for the family-friendly corporation. All of us are struggling to adapt to the new social realities such as balancing work and home demands, and work places are playing an increasingly important role in helping employees meet their family roles. The more equipped employees and employers are, through practical books such as this one, the greater the possibilities are for achieving healthy and productive work places and communities.

Acknowledgments

I want to credit those who contributed to the value and usefulness of this work. To them I owe a debt of thanks. Any shortcomings herein are of my own making.

I am grateful to the many older people and family caregivers I have known and worked with over the years. I am especially indebted to Frank J. Manning, founder of the Massachusetts Association of Older Americans (MAOA), and to his successor, Elsie Frank. They provided inspiration and encouraged me to learn about aging and to take an active role in improving the situations of elders and their families. For their support, guidance, and instruction at various points in my career, I also want to thank Jon Pynoos, Robert Morris, and Val Halamandaris.

Special thanks go to the critical readers of various chapters: Jim Murphy, Niels Nielsen, and Scott Meis. I am also grateful to the dear friends who encouraged this project from its earliest days and who provided advice and assistance along the way: Hannah Benoit, Bob Lavelle, Tom Allen, Thom and Joann Marosy, and Michelle Marosy. I also appreciated the help of John T. Harney, who offered much needed and appreciated guidance in the preparation of the original manuscript.

Gail Hunt, Donna Wagner, Brad Googins, Margaret Neal, and Sally Coberly provided special assistance and insights. Cliff Hakim gets credit for helping me to rethink the meaning of work. I am also grateful to the following people for giving generously of their time and sharing their perspectives in the preparation of this book: Lorraine Brozyna, Joan Butler-West, Paul Raia, Dan O'Leary, Alan Frohman, Skip Schlenk, Ellen Barkan, John Place, Diane Piktialis, Bruce Davidson, Debra Dwork, Kathy Hazzard, Suzanne Mintz, Neal Winston, Kathy Partridge, Tom Pugh, Lynn Fetterolf, Angela Heath, Margaret Neal, Scott Bass, Richard Griffin, Bill Conway, Irma Tetzloff, Abby Steele, Nancy Kaplan, Kathleen O'Laughlin, Judith Gonyea, Cyndie White, Linda Sterthaus, Donna Wagner, Lucia De Venere, Eric Sokol, Claire Scott, and Cheryll Schramm.

I reserve final, heartfelt thanks to my loving wife Donna and son Martin, whose understanding and willingness to sacrifice precious time together made it possible for me to complete this work.

Introduction

At my age I stand, as it were, on a high peak alone. I have no contemporaries with whom I can exchange memories or views. But that very isolation gives me a less biased view of that vast panorama of human life which is spread before the eyes of a centenarian, still more when those eyes are the eyes of an archaeologist. It is true that much of the far distance is shrouded in cloud and mist, but every here and there, the fog thins a little and one can see clearly the advance of mankind.

    —Dr. Margaret Murky in her autobiography, *My First Hundred Years*

In the summer of 1985, a small group of home health care managers met at the Center for Home Health Development in Princeton, New Jersey, to plan a conference entitled, "You Hired My Family, Too!" They saw the need for a closer connection between the world of work and the world of care of elders in their homes. They had heard powerful stories from the nurses, social workers, therapists, and home care aides who worked in their home care agencies. They told of sons and daughters making remarkable sacrifices to help their ailing parents continue to live at home while they struggled to fulfill their work responsibilities.

The conference drew a capacity crowd, with human resource professionals traveling from all over the United States to attend. At the time, corporate elder care was being touted as the "employee benefit of the 1990s." Newspaper and magazine headlines announced the pioneering efforts of IBM, The Travelers Company, Johnson & Johnson, and a handful of other large corporations that were investing in helping workers balance work and family responsibilities, including the care of older relatives.

What the conference attendees found most valuable by far were the life experiences shared by a panel of employee caregivers themselves. Until they had a chance to hear and discuss the personal stories of the workers who joined them that day, these business leaders regarded elder care as an abstraction, just so much statistical and gerontological jargon.

The typical family member, alas, relates to elder care in the same way. For most people, helping parents or other older relatives remains an abstraction, a notion they do not particularly want to entertain, until some change in circumstances in the elder's life creates or dramatizes need. Then, they view the situation as a crisis.

The need for managers to understand elder care continues today. Surveys established over a decade ago that a lack of understanding of employee caregiver needs is the number one reason employers have not taken action to address elder care as a work place issue.

MANAGERS AND ELDER CARE

This book is written for the oft-maligned, underappreciated, overworked manager who oversees the day-to-day work of others. Everything seems to land on the manager's desk . . . or in the seat next to it! Increasingly, the pile of work on the manager's desk includes work/life conflicts—their own and those of their coworkers.

Managers often have more power and influence than they realize. The most powerful means by which they can influence others is the example they set by their behavior. A single-focus attention to work duties can lead the manager to adopt a truncated, unidimensional view of life. In extreme cases, some managers sadly convince themselves that their very purpose for being is tied exclusively to the success of the enterprise by which they are employed. Such neglect of the inner self can hamper recognition of coworkers as fellow human beings and lead to an unhappy existence.

Fortunately, the messy and often emotionally intense issues like raising children, falling in and out of love, and coping with aging and the needs of aging parents continue to insert themselves into the work lives of managers, providing reminders of their humanity, and opportunities to grow as caring persons. Self-care and caring for others is healthy and requires time and energy. Managers can help create healthy work environments that acknowledge this reality.

Dealing with the issues of aging (like the needs of working caregivers described in this book) is a matter of self-interest. Over the next forty years, the number of Americans over age 85 will triple to 12 million people *and every one of them is alive today.* The baby boomers are about to create a grandparent boom . . . and a great-grandparent boom.

Despite the reality of the graying of America, today's managers receive little formal training or education in gerontology. Consequently, managers cannot be expected to deal effectively with the challenges generated by the unprecedented aging of the population. This book is intended to help fill this gap in gerontological knowledge for management generalists.

THE NEW COMPETITIVE REALITY

Three trends fuel the need for today's managers to develop an understanding of and ability to effectively deal with the issues presented by working caregivers: (1) the New Competitive Reality, and the way it has changed the role of the manager; (2) the aging of the population; and (3) the New Social Contract for Working.

The world of work has changed dramatically since 1985. The New Competitive Reality, driven by deregulation of many industries, increased global competition, technological advances, and the pressure for short-term results, requires organizations and the managers within them to adapt to change more quickly, and to do more with less. Corporate downsizing and reengineering have accelerated in the 1990s, creating a climate of uncertainty and work place insecurity.

Managers are feeling the affects of work place changes as acutely as anyone. People in the middle levels of most organizations have very difficult jobs. Many businesses have eliminated or are eliminating layers of management. According to one study, one-third of all middle management jobs were eliminated in the purge that accompanied the first wave of downsizing in the late 1980s.[1] The remaining middle managers have more crossfunctional responsibilities. Often, human resources staffing has been pared back.

The owner of a small manufacturing or service firm faces the same demands related to the trends cited here as an administrator at a Fortune 500 company. Small business has always needed to be adaptable and quick on its feet in order to survive and thrive. This is as true today as ever.

THE AGING OF THE POPULATION

Every month, 30,000 Americans turn 65, enough people to fill a baseball stadium the size of Boston's Fenway Park. The youth culture that sprang to life in the sixties with the coming of age of the baby boomers began to give way to the Mature Market in 1996 when the first of the boomers turned 50. A few years earlier, the number of Americans over age 50 surpassed the number of teenagers for the first time in history.

The fastest-growing age group of all? People over age 85. These are the people most likely to need help with tasks of everyday living, like bathing, dressing, toileting, and cooking. A person who is 85 years old is twice as likely to need help with one of these activities of daily living as his or her counterpart who has just reached age 65.

Family members provide the vast majority of the help needed by elders. Only about 20 percent of home care is provided by agencies or paid personnel. Wives, daughters, daughters-in-law, nieces, granddaughters, husbands, sons, and nephews are, collectively, providing over $300 billion worth of care on an informal, unpaid basis.

These are the working caregivers. There are over 14 million of them today. Their numbers are growing and will continue to grow.

THE NEW SOCIAL CONTRACT FOR WORKING

The changing business environment and the graying of America provide a backdrop for a third major shift taking place in society: the changing meaning of work itself.

The old social contract for working provided a sense of security and also fostered worker dependence on the employer. Under the old rules of the game, the employer's obligations included providing job security and expanding pay, benefits, and career opportunities. Jobs were clearly defined, closely directed, and supervised. Today, that old contract has been broken. According to career counselor Cliff Hakim, "Dependence on the organization is obsolete. . . . Loyalty to the organization no longer guarantees job security. Today, and for the foreseeable future, people's employability lies in their own hands."[2] Employers value skills and performance over loyalty and tenure.

At the same time, the Families and Work Institute cites "mounting evidence that U.S. workers are changing what they want from a work experience. They want more meaningful work. They want more control over their hours and more flexibility in how work gets done. They want a better quality of life and their employer's recognition of them as a whole person."[3] The study points to demographic change and today's faster pace of life as contributing to workers' need for "satisfying, flexible work that allows for some semblance of a personal life."[4]

To be effective, today's manager must find a way to resolve these conflicting forces in the work place to provide the support needed to unleash the potential of workers, so that they may contribute their best effort on the job. Elder care needs existed for workers before major corporate downsizing began in the late 1980s; millions more face elder care related needs today. The key is to understand these individual needs that affect motivation and job performance.

A FRAMEWORK FOR UNDERSTANDING AND ACTION

This book provides a framework for understanding working caregivers' needs and for creating a work environment that provides options to allow these workers to continue to work productively. In addition, it describes the practical steps that a manager can take on an individual basis, whether or not the organization embraces work/family balance as a key component of its corporate culture.

Chapter 1 focuses on why elder care is a growing work place issue, highlighting who the caregivers are, business costs related to elder caregiving, and the prevalence of elder care as an employee benefit.

Chapter 2 provides specific guidance on preparing to address elder care and work issues from both individual and organizational perspectives. It includes exercises that allow managers to measure their "aging IQ" and to assess their views on managing a family-friendly work place. A description of the Pyramid of Work/Life Needs gives managers a framework for planning work/life strategic initiatives that include elder care.

The wide-ranging needs of working caregivers are examined in Chapter 3, under the headings of Time, Timely Information, Finances, and Emotional Support. Caregivers are a heterogeneous group. Therefore, this chapter also highlights characteristics of segments of the working caregiver population, showing some of the ways in which the needs of male and female caregivers, long distance caregivers, and racial and ethnic minorities differ from caregivers in general. Finally, a comparison of child care and elder care needs provides insight for program development.

Chapter 4 provides guidance and suggestions for dealing with elder care issues on the individual, one-to-one level. Case examples illustrate how the manager can apply basic principles of sound management to prevent and successfully resolve work/family conflicts related to elder care by using a simple, four-step process.

Chapter 5 begins by answering the question, "Why make an investment in developing an elder care response?" The remainder of the chapter deals with responding to elder care needs on the organizational level. Using a seven-step process, managers learn to match the needs of working caregivers to programs that will alleviate productivity losses. Topics covered include quantifying the need for elder care help, organizing training and education sessions, and evaluating potential elder care service vendors. Specific techniques for evaluating the cost effectiveness of elder care initiatives are included.

The last chapter examines the options available for organizational response and includes definitions of the many forms of flexible work arrangements, as well as policies and benefits. Corporate profiles and model program descriptions round out the presentation.

Reference Information

The five appendices include descriptions of the major federal programs for older Americans with contact information and a sample survey questionnaire form. An annotated bibliography includes resources helpful to managers, as well as a list of suggested titles for inclusion in a work place caregivers library. Finally, a glossary of elder care acronyms and abbreviations will serve as a handy reference source for managers seeking to integrate work place programs with the activities of community agencies and government programs.

LANGUAGE AND AGING

The words we use can aid or hinder our understanding of the phenomenon of aging. The term *elder* is employed throughout the text because to me it connotes essential respect for the person who has survived to the Third Age. While *old person* may convey the truth of a person's chronological status, it fails to convey an individual's essential social dimension, that is, one's link to younger generations. *Elder* is a crossgenerational term. *Senior citizen, retiree*, and *the elderly*, perpetuate a view of the elder as different from others, somehow separate from the life of society as a whole. These terms reinforce the stereotypes that further ageism—prejudice and discrimination against elders.

NOTES

1. Charles Handy, *The Age of Unreason* (Cambridge, Mass.: Harvard Business School Press, 1989), 91.
2. Clifford Hakim, *We Are All Self-Employed—The New Social Contract for Working in a Changed World* (San Francisco: Berrett Koehler, 1994), 21.
3. Deborah K. Holmes and Dana E. Friedman, *The Changing Employer–Employee Contract: The Role of Work-Family Issues.* Conference Report, Families and Work Institute, New York, 1995.
4. Holmes and Friedman, *Changing Contract*, 1.

A MANAGER'S GUIDE TO ELDER CARE AND WORK

Chapter 1

Why Elder Care Is a Work Place Issue

Anyone can become a caregiver at a moment's notice. All it takes is a stroke, an accident, or a debilitating illness—and someone you love.
—Suzanne Mintz,
President, National Family Caregivers Association

When a parent becomes sick or disabled, one's life changes. The exact set of changes that takes place depends on a myriad of circumstances, including individual life history. Interactions with spouses, siblings, parents, and to a degree, coworkers, shape individual identity and influence how one deals with an elder family member's mental or physical frailty. The need for caregiving assistance is itself often rooted in one or more chronic illnesses and related impairments which can take many forms. Consequently, for any given individual, elder caregiving can involve a wide range of circumstances and can have varying degrees of impact on work place performance.

CAREGIVER DEFINED

There is no universally accepted definition of the term caregiver. For the purposes of this book, the term caregiver is used to mean an "informal," that is, unpaid, provider of physical, financial, or emotional support for a relative or loved one whose activities of daily living are limited due to loss of mental or physical function. Caregiving responsibilities may include providing direct personal care, as well as finding and managing supplemental care in the community.[1]

A working caregiver is one who is engaged in paid employment on a full- or part-time basis. Working caregivers may, of course, work for others or be self-employed.

Physical, Financial, and Emotional Support

The term "caregiver" might conjure up an image of a daughter or son taking a frail mother or father by the arm and helping him or her down the front steps of the family home and into a car to go grocery shopping. In this example, the caregiver is obviously providing physical help to assure the elder's safety, but the assistance may also include financial support if that person pays the grocery bill. Perhaps the walk down the front steps was preceded by a half-hour talk at the kitchen table during which time the caregiver simply listened to the parent express feelings of sadness and confusion since the recent loss of a spouse. Clearly, the incident would then also include an element of emotional support.

An elder's needs may require a varying range of physical care; for example, help may be necessary with dressing, grooming, and bathing, or, in the case of a more severely disabling condition, assistance with toileting and transferring in and out of bed. A person with late-stage Alzheimer's Disease will need continuous supervision, including physical intervention to prevent injury due to wandering or self-abusing behavior. Many forms of caregiving will obviously be physically exhausting.

Some caregivers function mainly as planners and organizers of care. Sometimes, given the realities of contemporary family and work life, this is done on a long-distance basis. Trying to arrange needed home care help for an ailing parent three thousand miles away will likely be a frustrating, anxiety-provoking, and time-consuming experience.

Cost Concerns

The cost of long-term care may well threaten a family's financial security. The cost of paying for nursing home care at $3,000 to $7,000 per month can quickly eliminate an elder's life savings. Few working people are able to long sustain this level of expense for a loved one's care.

Surveys have shown that a majority of Americans believe that the federal Medicare program covers the cost of long-term care.[2] In fact, Medicare pays only for short-term rehabilitative care at home or in a nursing home for individuals who have a medical condition that can be shown to be improving. For most chronic conditions, the goal is care, not cure, and Medicare will not pay for what it defines as "custodial" care. Medicaid, a state–federal program for low income elders and disabled persons, as well as families receiving public assistance, will pay for long-term care and is the single largest payment source for nursing home care today. Because of increasingly restrictive federal rules about transfer of assets from parents to children, however, fewer elders will be deemed eligible for Medicaid. As the federal government moves to limit its spending on Medicaid, accordingly the financial burden of paying for care is shifting to the states, which in turn are restricting eligibility. These changes effectively shift more of the cost of care to elders' life savings or to family members. Many of the latter are the working caregivers with whom this book is concerned.

The Relative or Loved One

Spouses or parents are most commonly the care receivers. However, working caregivers may also be involved with caring for other family members, close friends, or even neighbors.

While this book focuses on the needs of working caregivers who are assisting older persons, the fact should be noted that 75 percent of all persons with chronic illnesses are under sixty-five years of age. A young mother whose child is born with a severe physical disability can face the same or higher levels of stress as the middle-aged worker whose mother has had a disabling stroke. The mental and physical burden of providing in-home care for a son or daughter with AIDS can be overwhelming. In 1994, one in seven working-age adults—23 million men and women—was limited in activities by a chronic condition. Almost 5 million children had activity-limiting chronic conditions.[3]

How Many Working Caregivers Are There?

In 1996, the National Alliance for Caregiving conducted a national survey and concluded that there are an estimated 22,411,200 American households with English-speaking caregivers.[4] Close to two in three caregivers (64%) are working, 52 percent full-time and 12 percent part-time. This translates into 14.4 million full- and part-time employed caregivers. This exceeds the findings of a 1994 report by the U.S. General Accounting Office (GAO), which estimated that about 8 million working Americans have parents or spouses who are disabled and may need assistance with activities of daily living.

In their article on use of work place programs by employed caregivers, Wagner and Hunt summarized research findings to date regarding prevalence of elder caregiving as a work place issue.[5] They point out that while some employee surveys have found that between 23 percent and 32 percent of respondents indicate involvement in elder caregiving, reports from employers offering elder care programs indicate a use rate of roughly 1 percent to 4 percent of a given work force. They cite a meta-analysis of seventeen employee surveys by Gorey, Rice, and Brice which concludes that a more accurate estimate of employee caregiving would be between 7.4 percent and 11.8 percent of the work force.[6]

Most Caregivers Are Middle-Aged Women

Most elder caregiving support is provided by women. Indeed, nearly three-quarters (73%) of all caregivers are women.[7] However, as the traditional breadwinner–housekeeper male–female roles continue to change, a significant number of men are taking on elder caregiving responsibilities as well. Figure 1.1 shows the relative proportion of female and male relatives caring for older persons.

Caregivers come from every walk of life and from every social and economic strata. The proportion of caregivers in black and Asian households tends to be higher than among Hispanic and white households (see Table 1.1). This is a particularly significant fact in light of population projections that show that the older population and the American work force are becoming more racially and ethnically diverse. In 1994, one in ten older Americans were of a racial or ethnic background other than white. In 2050, this proportion is expected to rise to two in ten. Similarly, the proportion of elders who are Hispanic is expected to climb from 4 percent to 16 percent over the same period.[8]

The National Alliance for Caregiving survey found that about 9 percent of caregivers have less than a high school education, and 35 percent are high school graduates, while over more than half (52%) have at least some college. Caregivers are an economically diverse lot as well: Table 1.2 shows that 14 percent come from households with annual incomes of under $15,000, and almost 11 percent come from households with incomes over $75,000. The median household income is $35,000.

Figure 1.1
Most Caregivers Are Women

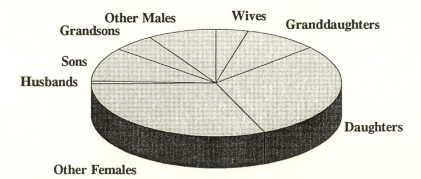

Source: National Alliance for Caregiving (NAC) and the American Association of Retired Persons (AARP), *Family Caregiving in the U.S.: Findings from a National Survey* (Washington, D.C.: NAC and AARP, 1997).

Table 1.1
Number and Percentage of Caregivers in U.S. Households by Race and Ethnic Background

Households	% of Households	Number of Households
White, Non-Hispanic	82.6%	18,290,000
Black, Non-Hispanic	10.8%	2,380,000
Hispanic	4.8%	1,050,000
Asian	1.8%	400,000
Total	**100%**	**22,120,000**

Source: National Alliance for Caregiving (NAC) and the American Association of Retired Persons (AARP), *Family Caregiving in the U.S.: Findings from a National Survey* (Washington, D.C.: NAC and AARP, 1997).

Among working caregivers, one study showed that executive-level managers reported a higher incidence of elder caregiving responsibilities than other workers. To find out how corporations and their employees deal with elder care, *Fortune* magazine and John Hancock Financial Services sponsored two surveys, one of executives and one of nonexecutive workers in Fortune 500 companies. Of the executives who completed questionnaires, 91 percent held

Table 1.2
Percentage of Households with Caregivers by Annual Income Level

Household Income	% of Households
Under 15,000	0.14
15,000 - 39,900	41.3%
40,000 - 74,900	24.3%
75,000 or higher	10.9%
Total	**90.5%**

Source: National Alliance for Caregiving (NAC) and the American Association of Retired Persons (AARP), *Family Caregiving in the U.S.: Findings from a National Survey* (Washington, D.C.: NAC and AARP, 1997).

posts in top management, including 58 percent with titles of either CEO, President, or Chairman. The findings were that while 37 percent of workers have been personally responsible for providing care for elderly persons in the past two years, fully 49 percent of corporate executives have experienced elder care responsibilities as well.[9]

TRENDS FUELING THE GROWTH OF ELDER CARE NEEDS

Americans are living longer lives and the number of older people is increasing at a rate never before seen. Most of these elders are reasonably healthy and live quite independently. The number needing assistance will continue to increase. At the same time, more women, the traditional family caregivers, are in the work force. Consequently, there are fewer middle-aged family members at home seeing to the care of children or dependent older relatives. More working Americans are faced with the compelling demands of balancing child care and elder care responsibilities and work requirements. The demand for heightened productivity further squeezes the time available to workers trying to address essential family responsibilities. Americans are working longer hours and taking more work home. With the coming of age of the baby boom generation, the issues of elder caregiving are certain to increase in magnitude in the years to come.

The Graying of America

As suggested, a growing number of people are living into their eighties and nineties. In fact, over 25,000 Americans have reached their one-hundredth birthday. Hayflick cites Census data that shows that since 1950, the number of sixty-five-year-olds has doubled, the number of eighty-five-year-olds has quintupled, and the number of centenarians has increased tenfold.[10] Growth of the older population in the United States has outpaced the under-sixty-five population since 1900, and is projected to continue through the next century. Figures 1.2 and 1.3 show the relative rates of growth of two segments of the older population.

Figure 1.2 shows that since 1900 the percentage of "younger" old, or those age sixty-five to eighty-four, has grown and will continue to grow at a fairly steady rate. Figure 1.3 shows that the number of "very old" Americans (i.e., those over age eighty-five) has accelerated since 1960 and will continue to climb, as a percentage of the total population, through the year 2040 when the baby boomers reach this age. As we will discuss, this phenomenal, unprecedented growth in the number of very old Americans has particular relevance to the emergence of elder care as a work place issue.

What accounts for this growth in the number of older Americans? While gains in life expectancy in the first half of this century came largely from decreased mortality rates for infectious diseases among children and young adults in the United States, the additional gains since 1950 have resulted from

Figure 1.2
Percentage of Population Aged 65 to 84, 1900–2040

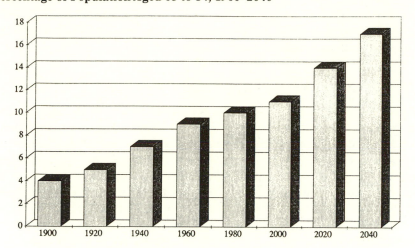

Source: U.S. Bureau of the Census, *Current Population Reports, Population Projections of the U.S. by Age, Sex, Race and Hispanic Origin, 1993-2050*, by Jennifer Cheeseman Day (Washington, D.C.: U.S. Government Printing Office, 1993), 25–1104.

Figure 1.3
Percentage of Population Over 84, 1900–2040

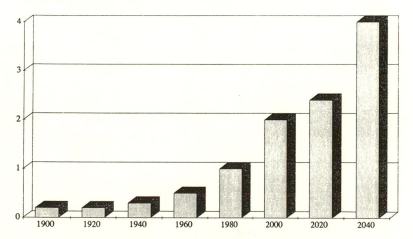

Source: U.S. Bureau of the Census, *Statistical Brief: Sixty-Five Plus in the United States* (Washington, D.C.: U.S. Government Printing Office, 1995).

lower mortality rates of chronic diseases in older adults. In other words, older Americans with chronic conditions, like heart disease, diabetes, arthritis, and high blood pressure, are living longer than ever before. In addition, American families are having fewer children, resulting in a lower birth rate. A woman born in 1900 could expect to live to about forty-eight years of age, and a man to age forty-six. Today, life expectation at birth is about seventy-five years.[11] The combination of increased life expectancy and a lower average birth rate has resulted in an increase in the size of the older population relative to the U.S. population as a whole.

Very Old Americans Are More Likely to Need Care

Most older people are physically active, able to care for themselves, and not in need of long-term care. However, the likelihood of an older person needing assistance rises sharply with advancing age. Only about 14 percent of people aged sixty-five to seventy-four are disabled, but that proportion rises to over 50 percent for people aged eighty-five and over—and this is the fastest growing age group in society.[12] Figure 1.4 illustrates how the percentage of persons needing assistance with everyday activities increases with age. There are about 3.5 million persons over eighty-five alive today. With the aging of the baby boomers, the number of Americans over age eighty-five will nearly quadruple to over 12 million by 2040.[13] Between 1990 and 2030, the elder population in need of assistance with activities of daily living will double, from 7 million to 14 million.[14] Largely because women live longer than men, the disabled elderly are disproportionately very old widows.

Figure 1.4
Need for Personal Assistance Increases with Age

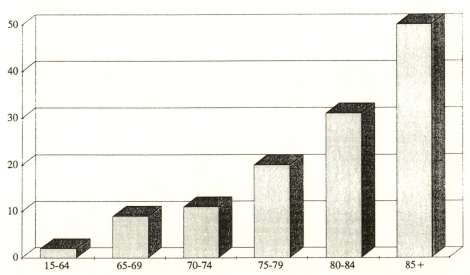

Source: U.S. Bureau of the Census, *Statistical Brief: Sixty-Five Plus in the United States* (Washington, D.C.: U.S. Government Printing Office, 1995).

More Women in the Work Force

More women are working outside the home today than at any other time in American history. Today there are more than 55 million women in the work force in the United States, or some 46 percent of the total work force. As Figure 1.5 shows, the number of women in the work place has increased from 31.5 million to 56.6 million between 1970 and 1990.

In fact, 55 percent of women are working outside the home today, and this percentage is expected to continue to increase.[15] This is clearly a significant development for the provision of elder care in America, given women's traditional role in providing unpaid elder care within families. Most of the women joining the work force have been between the ages of twenty-five and thirty-five. As these working women continue to age, the likelihood increases of their having to deal simultaneously with child-rearing and elder care.

BUSINESS COSTS RELATED TO ELDER CAREGIVING

The cost to U.S. businesses in decreased productivity of employees with caregiving responsibilities is at least $11.4 billion per year, according to a 1997 report by MetLife and the National Alliance for Caregiving.[16] Table 1.3 shows the component costs of this estimate.

This estimate conservatively states the costs to American business because it includes only caregivers who work full-time and provide assistance with at least two Activities of Daily Living, like bathing, feeding, toileting, transfer-

Figure 1.5
Men and Women in the Work Force, 1970–1990 (in Millions)

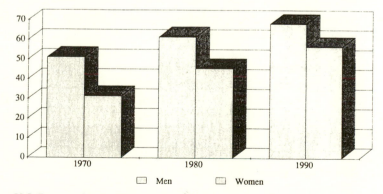

□ Men   □ Women

Source: U.S. Bureau of Labor Statistics, *Workplace Diversity*, by Katharine Esty et al. (Washington, D.C.: U.S. Government Printing Office, 1995).

Table 1.3
Annual U.S. Employer Costs for Working Caregivers

	Men	Women	Total
Replacing employees who quit	$1,630,533,866	$3,303,262,439	$4,933,796,305
Absenteeism	131,399,945	266,196,973	397,596,918
Partial Absenteeism	161,375,557	326,923,158	488,298,715
Workday Interruptions	1,244,317,663	2,520,804,670	3,765,122,333
Elder Care Crises	358,363,487	725,991,745	1,084,355,232
Supervision of Personal Caregiv	266,084,889	539,048,871	805,133,760
Total Costs	3,792,075,407	7,682,227,856	11,474,303,263

Source: MetLife and the National Alliance for Caregiving, *The MetLife Study of Employer Costs for Working Caregivers* (Westport, Conn.: MetLife, 1997).

ring from bed to chair or walking, and at least four Instrumental Activities of Daily Living, like financial management, transportation, help with medications, shopping, or preparing meals. Over 48 percent of all employed caregivers work part-time, and there are at least 8.7 million working caregivers who provide less intensive forms of help, including long-distance caregiving. In addition, this estimate does not include increased costs of health and mental health care for caregivers, leaves of absence, reduced hours of work, transfers to less demanding jobs, or turning down promotions because of caregiving responsibilities. If all these additional costs were included, the total costs to U.S. businesses would exceed $29 billion per year.[17]

Per Caregiver Costs Average $1,141 to $3,200 Annually

The $1,141 estimated cost per employee used in the MetLife study is similarly conservative. A 1994 study of one large (86,000 salaried employees) manufacturing company estimates total costs related to personal caregiving at $5,464,436, or nearly $3,200 per employee caregiver.[18] Like the 1997 MetLife study, this study also excluded the large number of caregivers who may oversee care of a relative but who do not provide personal, hands-on care. Other studies estimate that productivity losses related to elder caregiving cost employers $2,500 to $3,100 per year per employed caregiver.[19]

Three Basic Cost Areas

Employers' measurable costs associated with elder caregiving fall into three basic categories: employee productivity, management–administrative costs, and health care, including mental health. The cost components within each category are listed below:

Employee Productivity

• Replacement of employees who burn out while on the job, or who terminate.
• Absenteeism.
• Partial absenteeism (e.g., arriving late for work or leaving early, extended lunch breaks).
• Workday interruptions (e.g., time spent making phone calls to the care recipient or to service providers, receiving phone calls, or being distracted from work in other ways).

These costs are often related to the elder care crises (e.g., the parent goes into the hospital or has a severe health care crisis, or the older person's residence must be moved).

Management–Administration

There are costs associated with supervising personnel who are personal caregivers. These include additional hours of supervisory time and the impact of additional stress on managers and supervisors who are often ill-equipped to manage the personnel and productivity issues related to workers' caregiving responsibilities.

Health–Mental Health Care

• Costs for caregivers under a physician's care.
• Costs associated with treatment for anxiety and depression.
• Employee Assistance Program costs.

In addition to the three basic categories of costs listed, there are a number of working caregiver costs that the literature identifies but for which researchers lack easily quantifiable costs. These costs include

• *Leaves of Absence.* Studies indicate that 9 percent and 11 percent respectively of employed caregivers took a leave of absence from work due to caregiving at some point during the time they were caregivers.[20]
• *Reducing Work Schedules or Changing Jobs.* Several studies report that between 5 percent and 17 percent of respondents said that they had reduced from full- to part-time work or changed jobs or attempted to change jobs due to caregiving–work conflicts.[21]
• *Loss of Human Capital.* Examples include turning down promotions, transfers, extra projects, missing meetings and business trips, and reducing continuing education.

These impacts represent substantial negative but unquantifiable "job opportunity" costs for both employee and employer.

The prevalence of elder caregiving as a work place issue and its cost to employers is likely to rise with the aging of the population.

PREVALENCE OF ELDER CARE AS
AN EMPLOYEE BENEFIT

As demonstrated, employers are clearly bearing significant costs related to working caregivers. How many employers have responded by including specific programs, policies, or benefits intended to address elder care concerns?

Studies conducted by employee benefit consulting firms indicate that an increasing number of larger firms offer some form of elder care assistance.[22] About one-third of such firms offer elder care compared to 82 percent offering some form of child care.

In one of the few large scale studies which included employers of all sizes, the U.S. General Accounting Office found in 1994 that 2.6 million American workers, or about 3 percent of the work force, have access to an employer-sponsored elder care resource and referral service.[23] Work scheduling options, like leave without pay and flextime, are more commonly offered. Table 1.4 lists the top ten types of elder care-related benefits offered, and the estimated number of workers who had access to each.

Elder care assistance is most common in larger firms, certain industries, and in companies with child care benefits. As Figure 1.6 shows, companies in the communications, utilities, real estate, and insurance industries are more likely to offer elder care for employees.

THE CHANGING SOCIAL CONTRACT FOR WORK

Dynamic, ongoing changes are taking place in the work place, driven by new technology and the transformation to a global economy. These changes are changing the contract between employer and worker. This contract—commonly referred to as the "new deal"—has changed the understanding of what a company and its workers owe each other. For workers at every level, the former relationship between employer and employee, based on the presumption of employer-supplied job security in return for employee loyalty, has been replaced. Some of the characteristics of the new deal include

- no long-term commitment by either companies or employees.
- the need for employees to take responsibility for their own careers.
- movement from corporate paternalism to employee empowerment.
- employee–employer partnership.
- personal accountability.
- pay for performance.[24]

Critics of the new deal say that reengineering and restructuring fostered mistrust, heightened insecurity, and undermined loyalty in the world of work.

Table 1.4
Estimates of Access to Elder Care-Related Benefits in 1994 (in Millions of Employees)

Benefit Type	Estimated No.of Employee With Access
Leave without pay*	27.0
Dependent Care Reimbursement Plans	20.9
Paid sick leave	14.1
Temporary reduction in work hours	13.7
Counseling on legal, personal, or financial elder care issues	13.3
Flextime	12.4
Part-time employment with benefits	11.6
Job sharing	7.7
Compressed work schedule	7.4
Elder care reference materials	7.0

Source: U.S. General Accounting Office, *Long Term Care: Private Sector Elder Care Could Yield Multiple Benefits* (Washington, D.C.: U.S. General Accounting Office, 1994), 24.

*Data do not reflect impact of the federal Family and Medical Leave Act implemented in August 1993, which is estimated to cover 66 percent of all American workers.

Defenders insist that the changes, though painful in the short run, are essential for survival, and that they will position companies to seize new opportunities for growth in an increasingly competitive environment.

In this new environment, there is no single, new arrangement or relationship that fits all organizations. Each company must craft its own, and in some cases, several arrangements with different groups of workers in different business units. Where do life and family balance programs, like elder care, fit within this new business situation?

Conscious Loyalty

Hakim points out that today every worker has two jobs: his or her professional job and the job of career self-manager.[25] Since there is no automatic or "blind" loyalty binding the worker to the employer, the company must build conscious loyalty, a form of loyalty which supports the success of the individual as well as the organization. In this light, the manager's role is one of change agent and facilitator, providing leadership, support, and the access to

Figure 1.6
Percentage Offering Elder Care by Industry

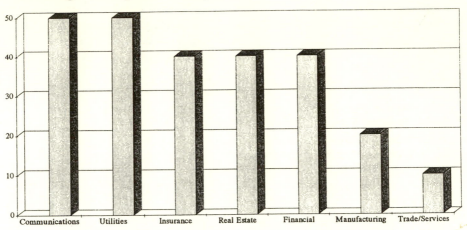

Source: U.S. General Accounting Office, *Long Term Care: Private Sector Elder Care Could
Yield Multiple Benefits* (Washington, D.C.: U.S. General Accounting Office, 1994), 13.

the resources that each worker needs to perform at his or her highest level.
The manager helps build conscious loyalty by supporting the worker's growth
and change in order to maintain employability. The quality of the organization's
entire work environment, including work/life balance initiatives, impacts the
manager's effectiveness as change agent and facilitator, and affects the
company's ability to attract and retain the best people in its industry.

Programs, policies, and resources that address elder care issues outside of
work enable workers to better focus their energy when they are at work. Elder
care offerings need to be developed as one component of a comprehensive
approach that recognizes the diverse needs of today's work force and workers' changing needs over time. Chapter 2 examines the factors that a manager
needs to consider in preparing such a comprehensive approach.

NOTES

1. The definition of the term caregiver varies among key research studies. The
definition used here draws on those found in Sally Coberly and Gail G. Hunt, *The
MetLife Study of Employer Costs for Working Caregivers* (Washington, D.C.: Wash-
ington Business Group on Health, 1995) and Margaret B. Neal, Nancy J. Chapman,
Berit Ingersoll-Dayton, and Arthur C. Emlen, *Balancing Work and Caregiving for
Children, Adults, and Elders* (Newbury Park, Calif.: Sage Publications, 1993).

2. American Association of Retired Persons (AARP), *Working Caregivers Report*
(Washington, D.C.: AARP, 1989).

3. Ellen Freudenheim, ed., *Chronic Care in America: A 21st Century Challenge*
(Princeton, N.J.: Robert Wood Johnson Foundation, 1996), 16.

4. National Alliance for Caregiving (NAC) and American Association of Retired Persons (AARP), *Family Caregiving in the U.S.: Findings from a National Survey* (Washington, D.C.: NAC and AARP, 1997), 8–11.

5. Donna L. Wagner and Gail G. Hunt, "The Use of Workplace Eldercare Programs by Employed Caregivers," *Research on Aging* 16, (1994): 69–84.

6. K. M. Gorey, R. W. Rice, and G. C. Brice, "The Prevalence of Elder Care Responsibilities among the Workforce Population," *Research on Aging* 14 (1992): 399–418.

7. NAC and AARP, *Family Caregiving*, 10.

8. Economics and Statistics Administration, U.S. Bureau of the Census, "Sixty-Five Plus in the U.S.," *Statistical Brief*, 2nd ed. (May 1995).

9. *Fortune* magazine and John Hancock Financial Services, *Corporate and Employee Response to Caring for the Elderly: A National Survey of U.S. Companies and the Work Force* (New York: *Fortune* magazine, 1989).

10. Leonard Hayflick, *How and Why We Age* (New York: Ballantine Books, 1994), 204.

11. Ibid., 66.

12. U.S. Bureau of the Census, "Projections of the Population of the United States by Age, Sex, and Race: 1983-2050," *Current Population Reports*, series P-25 (Washington, D.C.: U.S. Government Printing Office, 1984), Table 6.

13. U.S. Bureau of the Census, "Projections, 1990–2050," *Current Population Reports*, series P-25, no.1018 (Washington, D.C.: U.S. Government Printing Office, 1989).

14. The Pepper Commission, *A Call for Action: The Pepper Commission–U.S. Bi-Partisan Commission on Comprehensive Health Care, Final Report* (Washington, D.C.: U.S. Government Printing Office, 1990).

15. Katharine Esty, Richard Griffin, and Marcie Schorr Hirsch, *Workplace Diversity: A Manager's Guide to Solving Problems and Turning Diversity into a Competitive Advantage* (Holbrook, Mass.: Adams Media, 1995), 14.

16. Metropolitan Life Insurance Company, *The MetLife Study of Employer Costs for Working Caregivers* (Westport, Conn.: MetLife, 1997), 1.

17. Ibid., 7.

18. Coberly and Hunt, *The MetLife Study of Employer Costs*.

19. A. E. Scharlach, B. F. Lowe, and E. L. Schneider. *Elder Care and the Work Force: Blueprint for Action* (Lexington, Mass.: D.C. Heath, 1991).

20. A. E. Scharlach and S. L. Boyd. "Caregiving and Employment: Results of an Employee Survey," *The Gerontologist* 29 (1989): 382–387; AARP, *Working Caregivers Report*.

21. Ibid.

22. *Mercer Work/Life and Diversity Initiatives Benchmarking Survey 1996* (New York: William M. Mercer, 1996); Marie Lipari and Saline Leckman, *Work and Family Benefits Provided by Major U.S. Employers in 1996* (Lincolnshire, Ill.: Hewitt Associates, LLC, 1997).

23. U.S. General Accounting Office, *Long Term Care: Private Sector Elder Care Could Yield Multiple Benefits* (Washington, D.C.: U.S. General Accounting Office, 1994).

24. Ibid.

25. Cliff Hakim, "Building Conscious Loyalty," *The New Deal in Employment Relationships—A Council Report* (New York: The Conference Board, 1996), 19.

Chapter 2

Preparing to Address Elder Care and Work Issues

How can we be fully present to the elderly when we are hiding from our own aging? . . . Therefore, when speaking about caring in the context of aging, we want to speak first about caring as the way to the self before we speak about caring as the way to others.

—Henri J. M. Nouwen

It's the supervisor and the company's culture that really make the difference . . . if your company has flextime but your supervisor won't let you use it, it doesn't do you any good.

—Ellen Galinsky,
Co-President, Families and Work Institute

As with any important venture, it is wise to examine the prerequisites for success before embarking on development of an elder care initiative in the work place. A sailor assesses weather conditions and the seaworthiness of the vessel before shoving off on a journey; so too, the manager needs to examine certain key factors at play before launching into program planning.

This chapter provides a framework for the manager to examine individual readiness in terms of knowledge of and attitude about aging, caregiving and work/life balance issues, and the organization's readiness in terms of corporate culture and leadership support.

ASSESSING PERSONAL PREPAREDNESS

The most important element of mental readiness is one's attitude. *Webster's Collegiate Dictionary* defines attitude as one's "manner, disposition, feeling, position, etc. with regard to a person or thing; tendency or orientation, especially of the mind." The factors that shape one's attitudes include individual knowledge and life experiences and the culture within which one lives and works. The word attitude also implies that one has the ability to learn and make choices about how one works and lives. In order to make good choices in the area of elder care and work, managers need to examine their attitudes regarding aging and caregiving, and the legitimacy of accommodating workers' needs to balance personal and family obligations with job responsibilities.

Attitudes about Aging

The issues of working caregivers are intertwined with issues of aging. Everyone is aging, yet a great deal of what many people think they know about aging is actually based in hearsay or on commonly held myths about what it means to grow older.

From a strictly statistical perspective, the chances that any one individual will live until age eighty-five or older are higher now than at any other time in history. This means that in the course of a lifetime, the average person will probably need some help from others with activities of everyday living, such as cooking, cleaning, and getting dressed. Issues related to elder caregiving are not limited to such work place issues as productivity, supervision, and quality of work life. In addition to these important dimensions, the quality and availability of elder care is a matter of personal self interest for every member of society.

The image of an elder in failing health can stir up powerful feelings about aging and mortality. The way managers think and feel about their own aging can affect how they react to learning that someone who works with them is struggling with the burden of elder caregiving.

The Impact of Youth Culture

It is commonly recognized that American culture is youth oriented. With few exceptions, the images conveyed in advertising, on television, and in the movies reinforce the ideal of youth: active, slim, trim men and women, with nary a wrinkle in sight. Constant exposure to images of idealized youth results in an internalization of this notion of how we are "supposed to" look, feel, behave, and consume. The problem is that real life does not square with the image.

Jane Hyman points out that "Those of us who grew up knowing and loving our grandparents or other older people probably remember loving their wrinkled faces. In the years before we learned to think of the signs of age as 'unattractive,' a wrinkled face was often the most loving and the most beloved face we knew. However, as adults, we live in an environment in which standards of beauty are important, narrow, and restricted to the young."[1]

Continued exposure to age-biased commercials and other images can result in counterproductive beliefs about aging and about elders in general. Dr. Robert Butler, the first director of the National Institute on Aging, coined the term "ageism" in 1968 to describe prejudice and discrimination against elders. Ageism is as destructive a force as racial or gender discrimination. Like other forms of bigotry, ageism breeds in an environment of ignorance and misinformation. Perhaps the most corrosive aspect of ageism is its internal effect on the individual's self-image. The flip side of the sunny, idealized image of youth is the media's reinforcement of negative stereotypes of aging and older people: the "dirty old man"; the confused and befuddled older woman; the silly, superfluous little old lady who wants to know, "Where's the beef?"

Media images often belittle and trivialize elders rather than hold them in high regard as sources of wisdom and symbols of perseverance and strength. The result: many individuals become fearful of their own aging, afraid that they will become what they fear in their internally held image of the "Elder." In a caffeine-fueled work environment where everything has to be completed yesterday, it is easy to categorize elders as socially separate and "unproductive." Such stereotypical thinking can lead younger people to avoid older people and avoid thinking about aging, thus further separating themselves from the reality of aging and reinforcing prejudices and fears.

Knowledge about Aging and Caregiving

Is there a way to break the negative cycle of false assumptions, which create the biases that lead to thinking of elders as different and separate from others? What is the antidote to denial of aging? Is it fear of aging?

Increased knowledge of the aging process and establishing personal contact with older individuals can help break down barriers in thinking and behavior. The short Aging and Caregiving Quiz below provides a starting point toward a better understanding of aging.[2]

Aging and Caregiving Quiz

For each of the questions below, circle the answer you think comes closest to the truth. The correct answers to each of the twenty questions follow the quiz.

1. In general, old people tend to be pretty much alike.

    True   False

2. Over three-fourths of elders are healthy enough to carry out their normal activities.

    True   False

3. How much of the care provided to frail elders is rendered by family members on a voluntary basis, compared to care provided by agencies or professionals?

    a. 20 percent   b. 40 percent   c. 60 percent   d. 80 percent

4. The majority of old people feel miserable most of the time.

      True   False

5. Aging is a disease which results in deficits or impairments in optimal functioning of the human organism.

      True   False

6. Senility is a normal part of aging and, therefore, loss of mental capacity with aging is inevitable.

      True   False

7. Caregiving involves a role reversal between parent and child in which the adult child now "parents" the parent.

      True   False

8. Old people usually take longer to learn something new.

      True   False

9. The majority of older people are unable to adapt to change.

      True   False

10. An older woman is almost twice as likely to live in poverty as an older man.

      True   False

11. The majority of old people say they are seldom bored.

      True   False

12. In 1981, the average length of a hospital stay for an elder was 7.2 days. Today it is

      a. 5.5 days   b. 7.2 days   c. 10 days   d. 14 days

13. The majority of old people have no interest in, or capacity for, sexual relations.

      True   False

14. The majority of old people are socially isolated.

      True   False

15. Old people tend to become more religious as they age.

      True   False

16. More of the aged vote than any other age group.

      True   False

17. Participation in voluntary organizations (such as churches and clubs) tends to decline among the healthy aged.

      True   False

18. Older persons who reduce their activity tend to be happier than those who do not.

      True   False

19. Medicare pays for virtually all the health care needs of older Americans.

      True   False

20. After age 65, preventive health measures can have little impact on a person's overall health status.

      True   False

The correct answer for each question, along with a short discussion of the facts, is listed below. To calculate a score, assign five points for each correct answer.

1. *In general, old people tend to be pretty much alike.* Correct answer: False. Old people are not pretty much alike. There is at least as much variation among older people as there is at any age; there are the rich and the poor, happy and sad, healthy and sick, and those of high and low intelligence. In fact, some evidence indicates that as people age they become less alike and more heterogeneous on many dimensions. Each individual ages at his or her own rate, accumulating a lifetime of experiences, tastes and preferences, all of which help shape individual personality. Aging is less like a chute that everyone slides down at the same speed, and more like a set of stairs that each of us travels at a personal pace.

2. *Over three-fourths of elders are healthy enough to carry out their normal activities.* Correct answer: True. About 78 percent of the aged are healthy enough to engage in their normal activities. Most elders live independently in their own homes or apartments. Only about 5 percent of all persons over age 65 live in institutions like nursing homes; another 17 percent among those living in the community say they are unable to engage in their major activity (such as work or housework) because of chronic conditions. About 81 percent of those residing in the community have no limitations in their activities of daily living (e.g., eating, bathing, dressing, and toileting).

   However, 20 percent of those eighty-five years old and older live in institutions. The likelihood of a person living in an institution clearly increases with age.

3. *How much of the care provided to frail elders is rendered by family members on a voluntary basis, compared to care provided by agencies or professionals?* Correct answer: d. Over 80 percent. Family members provide the vast majority of the care for elders with mental and physical impairments. Called "informal" caregivers by elder care professionals, these family members deliver services estimated to be worth over $600 billion dollars per year if purchased directly. The "formal" caregiving network is comprised of home health agencies, nursing homes, hospice programs, hospitals, adult day health centers, social service agencies, visiting nurse associations, and other businesses and community organizations.

4. *The majority of old people feel miserable most of the time.* Correct answer: False. The majority of old people do not feel miserable most of the time. Studies of happiness, morale, and life satisfaction either find no significant differences among age groups, or find about 20 percent to 33 percent of elders score "low" on various happiness and morale scores. One study found only about 25 percent of persons sixty-five or older reporting that "This is the dreariest time of my life," while about half said "I am just as happy as when I was younger" and about 33 percent said "These are the best years of my life."

5. *Aging is a disease which results in deficits or impairments in optimal functioning of the human organism.* Correct answer: False. Aging itself is not a disease. To understand aging, we need to distinguish between normal aging and the diseases that are associated with old age. In the words of Dr. Leonard Hayflick, preeminent cell biologist and aging researcher: "No one has been hospitalized or has died from gray hair, wrinkled skin, or the inability to hear a high C! These nor-

mal changes that occur with aging are not diseases, but are typical of hundreds of thousands of similar though less apparent nondisease changes that occur throughout our bodies as we age. . . . We are not sick because we experience normal age changes. But the likelihood that we will get sick increases with age because the normal age changes make us more vulnerable to diseases that in youth would have been more easily repulsed."[3]

6. *"Senility" is a normal part of aging; loss of mental capacity with aging is inevitable.* Correct answer: False. The loss of mental capacity with age is not inevitable. Our own attitudes—about ourselves as aging persons and about others who have reached advanced age—play a major role in whether or not we continue to learn and remain mentally alert in later life. The maxim "use it or lose it" applies to many of our functions as we age, but especially to use of the brain. In the absence of a disease-related mental impairment, elders who read, do crossword puzzles, use computers, engage in stimulating discussions, and otherwise stretch their mental abilities can remain mentally sharp and "with it" for as long as they live.

    The forgetfulness and confusion seen in some elders may be associated with specific conditions, like severe depression or Alzheimer's disease. The presence of Alzheimer's disease increases from a rate of less than one-tenth of one percent among people aged sixty to sixty-five to as high as 47 percent among people over age eighty-five. Until recent publicity and research focused on Alzheimer's disease, public awareness of this disease was virtually nonexistent, and the erroneous assumption that "senility" was a normal consequence of aging was widespread.

7. *Caregiving involves a role reversal between parent and child in which the adult child now "parents" the parent.* Correct answer: False. The remark that "She is now parenting her parent" is a commonplace, generally accepted way of thinking about elder caregiving. It is also a dangerous way to view the change in relationship between adult child and ailing adult parent.

    While it is true that in a caregiving relationship, the adult child may begin to perform some tasks for an incapacitated parent that are similar to the tasks that parent performed for him or her in childhood, this does not constitute a reversal of the roles in their current relationship; rather, a healthy caregiving relationship is an adult-to-adult relationship.

    For the parent, it is denigrating to be treated like and spoken to as a child. Elders are adults and deserve to be treated as such, no matter how much or how little they can think or do for themselves. Each elder has a lifetime of experience and a wealth of time-tested opinions and has earned autonomy and pride. With the onset of a mental impairment, he or she may have reverted to "childish" ways, but that does not make the elder a child.

    For the caregiver, reversing the roles can only lead to frustration and increased stress. In her guide to caregiving, Virginia Morris provides this advice to caregivers: "If you try to parent your parent as you would a child, without perceiving the vast differences in the two situations, you will make things much harder for yourself. You will beat yourself up wondering why you are having such trouble with the task and you will be angry at your parent for not behaving more like a child."[4]

8. *Old people usually take longer to learn something new.* Correct answer: True. Elders usually do take longer to learn something new, compared with their own performances when they were younger or with performances of a younger co-

hort. However, much of the difference in the length of time it takes to learn something new can be explained by variables other than age, such as illness, motivation, learning style, and lack of practice. When these other variables are taken into account, chronological age does not provide a significant amount of influence on learning ability.

9. *The majority of older people are unable to adapt to change.* Correct answer: False. The majority of elders are able to adapt to change. It is clear that most older persons do change and adapt to the many changes that occur in old age, such as retirement, children leaving home, widowhood, moving to new homes, and serious illness. Their political and social attitudes also tend to shift with those of the rest of society and with approximately the same rate of change.

10. *An older woman is almost twice as likely to live in poverty as an older man.* Correct answer: True. The poorest groups in America are women over sixty-five living by themselves and women raising children alone. These two groups make up 70 percent of all poor people.[5] Among elders, poverty is concentrated among women and minorities. Over 15 percent of older women are poor, compared to about 8 percent of older men. Thirty-eight percent of black older women are poor. Twenty-five percent of older Hispanic women are poor. Twenty percent of women aged seventy-five or older are poor, and another 30 percent are near poverty. Men aged seventy-five and over by comparison have poverty rates of 10 percent and near-poverty rates of 16 percent.[6]

11. *The majority of old people say they are seldom bored.* Correct answer: True. The majority of old people do say they are seldom bored. In research studies, only 21 percent say that "Most of the things I do are boring or monotonous," and only 17 percent say that "not enough to do to keep me busy" is a problem for them. The Duke Longitudinal Study on Aging found that 87 percent said they had never been bored in the past week.

12. *In 1981, the average length of a hospital stay for an elder was 7.2 days. Today it is:* Correct answer: a. 5.5 days. Between 1981 and 1995, the average length of a hospital stay for Medicare beneficiaries fell by 23.6 percent from 7.2 to 5.5 days. Medical advances are speeding recovery and changes in the methods of reimbursement have also contributed to this decline in length of in-patient stays. Health care payors increasingly rely on less costly settings for recuperative care, including care in the patient's home and in subacute care facilities, such as specialized nursing homes. Elders are coming home from the hospital in frailer health, and family members are often involved in arranging needed post-hospital care.

13. *The majority of old people have no interest in, or capacity for, sexual relations.* Correct answer: False. The majority of persons past age sixty-five continue to have both interest in and the capacity to engage in sexual relations. Masters and Johnson found that the capacity for satisfying sexual relations usually continues into the decades of the seventies and eighties for healthy couples. The Duke University Longitudinal Studies found that sex continues to play an important role in the lives of the majority of men and women through the seventh decade of life. In other surveys, most elders have indicated that sex after sixty was as satisfying or more satisfying than when younger. Medication, illness, and societal mores may discourage sexual activity in some people over sixty. However, sexuality is very much a part of the later years.

14. *The majority of old people are socially isolated.* Correct answer: False. The majority of old people are not socially isolated. About two-thirds live with their spouses or family. Only about 4 percent of the elderly are extremely isolated, and most of these have had lifelong histories of withdrawal. Most elders have close relatives within easy visiting distance, and contacts between them are relatively frequent.

15. *Old people tend to become more religious as they age.* Correct answer: False. Older people do not tend to become more religious as they age. While it is true that the present generation of older persons tends to be more religious than the younger generations, this appears to be a generational difference rather than an aging effect, due to the older persons' more religious upbringing. In other words, members of the present older generation have been more religious all their lives rather than becoming more religious as they aged.

16. *More of the aged vote than any other age group.* Correct answer: False. Fewer of the aged vote than do middle-aged groups. For example, in the November 1990 election, voters aged fifty-five to sixty-four had the highest participation rate at 71 percent compared to 69 percent for those aged sixty-five to seventy-four, and 58 percent for those seventy-five and over. A crossnational study found the same pattern in Austria, India, Japan, and Nigeria.

17. *Participation in voluntary organizations (such as churches and clubs) tends to decline among the healthy aged.* Correct answer: False. Participation in voluntary organizations does not usually decline among healthy older persons. Several studies have shown that, when the effects of socioeconomic differences and health are controlled, age bears little or no relationship to voluntary association participation in middle age or later life. However, declining health does tend to decrease participation.

18. *Older persons who reduce their activity tend to be happier than those who do not.* Correct answer: False. Older persons who disengage from active roles do not tend to be happier than those who remain active. On the contrary, most recent studies have found that those who remain active tend to be happier than those who disengage.

19. *Medicare pays for virtually all the health care needs of older Americans.* Correct answer: False. While Medicare does cover short-term, acute medical expenses, like physician and hospital care, for persons over sixty-five, it does not pay for long-term care (i.e., nursing home care and in-home care over an extended period of time).

20. *After age sixty-five, preventive health measures can have little impact on a person's overall health status.* Correct answer: False. The good news about aging is that regular exercise, proper eating habits, and such behavior changes as stopping smoking can improve many parts of our lives. Healthy living habits can begin any time, and the results will be improved cardiovascular endurance, strengthened muscles, improved flexibility, increased sexual appetite, better sleeping, relief of daily tensions, and improved overall psychological functioning.

A score of seventy points or better on the Aging and Caregiving Quiz indicates a good grasp of some of the key facts about aging. A score below seventy indicates the need to take a closer look at one's assumptions and to gain more information.

Every month, researchers in the field of aging are uncovering new facts and insights about how we age. A better understanding of aging can enhance effectiveness as a supervisor and may even alleviate some of the anxiety a manager feels about his or her own future as an aging person. The books, videotapes, and publications listed in the Annotated Bibliography can provide that base of knowledge. Chapter 3 focuses on understanding the needs of working caregivers.

Attitudes about Work/Life Balance

In addition to examining attitudes and knowledge of aging, managers need to consider their views regarding balancing work and personal or family responsibilities. Over time, every manager develops certain attitudes and assumptions about work and how work is supposed to "fit" with other aspects of life. Influencing factors include the views of parents, early work experiences, role models, and the corporate cultures within which managers work. Management style reflects a manager's outlook on work/life balance questions.

The Work/Life Self-Assessment exercise below provides an opportunity for managers to consider their own views about allowing for balance of personal and work responsibilities. Based on the work of Magid and Codkind, the self-assessment is intended to stimulate self-reflection.[7] In completing the exercise, do not concentrate on trying to find the "right" or "wrong" answers. Instead, try to understand and reflect on the answers selected. The questions that follow the sixteen items are intended to stimulate self-reflection.

Manager's Work/Life Self-Assessment Exercise

After reading each item, circle one of the three choices: A for Agree; D for Disagree; or NA for Not Applicable.

1. It is reasonable to expect that work is the top priority in the lives of workers.

   A   D   NA

2. A worker requests permission for unanticipated time off. An appropriate first response is, "When will you return to work?"

   A   D   NA

3. It is acceptable to call in sick for a "mental health day."

   A   D   NA

4. It is acceptable to call in sick to visit a child's school.

   A   D   NA

5. Workers should be able to use a company's telephone lines to call elderly parents in another city.

   A   D   NA

6. Workers should be able to use a company's telephone lines to check on latchkey children.

     A   D   NA

7. Workers should be expected to call in daily from vacation and check phone mail on weekends and evenings.

     A   D   NA

8. Individuals who play an active role in parenting will probably not rise to the top at work.

     A   D   NA

9. The employee's value to the company depends on willingness and ability to travel, work overtime, and relocate.

     A   D   NA

10. The needs of the family are more important than the needs of the organization.

     A   D   NA

Magid and Codkind suggest these reflections on the answers selected:

- Are there significant responses above that may stand in the way of supporting employees' work and personal life choices? List those that come to mind.
- Do managers in the organization hold different values in regard to work–personal issues than those held by other workers?
- How would a manager identify such differences?

Increasing one's self-awareness regarding feelings and attitudes about work/life balance issues is the starting point for playing a supportive role as a manager or supervisor. See the Annotated Bibliography for additional sources of information to enhance self-awareness and develop an effective management style for dealing with the variety of work/life issues that arise in today's work place. Chapter 4 presents specific techniques that a manager can use when confronted with elder care-related work/life balance conflicts.

ASSESSING ORGANIZATIONAL PREPAREDNESS

The manager's assessment of the level of readiness of an organization to embrace an elder care initiative will involve looking at corporate culture as well as the resources available to support program planning and implementation.

"It is the supervisor and the company's culture that really make the difference," says Ellen Galinsky, Co-President of the Families and Work Insitute, a New York-based research and consulting firm. "Programs and policies are, in a sense, merely shells. It's how the supervisors use the shells that really counts. In other words, if your company has flextime but your supervisor won't let you use it, it doesn't do you any good."[8]

Elder Care and Corporate Culture

Every organization has a culture. *Webster's Collegiate Dictionary* defines culture as "the sum total of ways of living built up by a group of human beings and transmitted from one generation to another." Marvin Brower, for years the managing director of the McKinsey and Company management consulting firm, has defined the informal cultural elements of a business as "the way we do things around here." The organization's culture can either support or subvert activities intended to help workers balance the activities of their work and family lives.

Here are a few questions managers can ask to assess whether their organization's culture is family-friendly.

- Do the leaders of the organization regard balancing work and family responsibilities as an essential feature of working in the organization?
- Are the basic values of the organization stated in writing, and do they include respect for each individual worker?
- Does top management endorse, and equally important, personally participate in the implementation of work/family initiatives?
- Do managers "walk the talk?" For example, is it considered acceptable for a manager to make use of flex-time or a leave of absence to arrange care for his or her mother, or is elder care work flexibility just for "others," that is, nonmanagers?

Leadership Support

As discussed later in Chapter 4, respect for each individual working within the organization forms the foundation for self-directed work and for building trust among coworkers. Trust must exist for workers to feel comfortable about choosing options that allow them to balance their work and family lives. One of the clearest and most powerful ways for managers to build trust is through example. Conversely, one way to assure little or no utilization of elder care and other work/family supports is for management to send the subtle or not-so-subtle message that it's really not OK to make use of elder care family supports. Corporate cultural norms are built up over time, based on the behaviors of the men and women who work in the organization, especially those who hold positions of leadership.

Many managers of elder care programs point to the commitment of top management as one of the key factors in successful program development and implementation. Suzanne Mercure, manager of benefits planning at Bull Worldwide Information Systems, puts it this way: "It is extremely important to have the involvement and dedication of the CEO of the organization. [Our CEO] stands behind the program 100% and has given us the latitude to experiment."[9]

A 1996 study of work/family issues conducted by Googins of the Boston College Center on Corporate Community Relations for *Business Week* magazine found that, even among companies that have ostensibly embraced family-friendly values, there are mixed results. The report cites an example of one company that had recently instituted a host of such policies, programs, and practices. The company enthusiastically participated in the survey research which probed the attitudes and perceptions of both management and non-management workers. Executives anticipated positive results, perhaps recognition of the company as a model for other firms. They were stunned to see the results. While managers were patting themselves on the back for having implemented so many new options, workers reported a negative response to the initiatives, and little or no interest in making use of them. Why? The firm had recently completed a round of massive layoffs and workers perceived the new work/family initiatives as window-dressing. They reported that they were being asked to work more hours for lower pay in an atmosphere of fear and intimidation—hardly a corporate culture in which work/family balance can flourish.

Work/Life Pyramid of Needs

To be effective over time, initiatives for elder care in the work place need to be planted in the soil of a corporate culture that truly respects all its workers' responsibilities for fulfilling family obligations. The manager needs to include these issues in planning for every factor that bears on worker performance: job design, work processes, and organizational structure.

Figure 2.1 presents an organizational pyramid of needs, developed by Googins, as a way to think about work/life strategic initiatives. The basic values of respect for workers, balance, and flexibility form the three lower layers at the base of the pyramid. These values comprise the bedrock or foundation on which all other aspects of work/life initiatives are based. The small triangle at the peak of the pyramid includes the three p's usually included in a work/life initiative: programs, policies (including benefits), and practices. All the elements of an organization's work/life strategic initiative exist within an environment defined by the organization's culture, hence the spaces surrounding the diagram are labeled "culture."

The American psychologist Abraham Maslow devised a six-level hierarchy of motives, that, according to his theory, determine human behavior. Maslow ranks human needs as follows: (1) physiological; (2) security and safety; (3) love and feelings of belonging; (4) competence, prestige, and esteem; (5) self-fulfillment; and (6) curiosity and the need to understand.

Campbell and Koblenz liken the work and life pyramid of needs to Maslow's hierarchy of needs and suggest that the framework of needs presented in the pyramid depicts a new paradigm in addressing work/life issues that "enhances

Figure 2.1
Work and Life Strategic Initiative: Pyramid of Needs

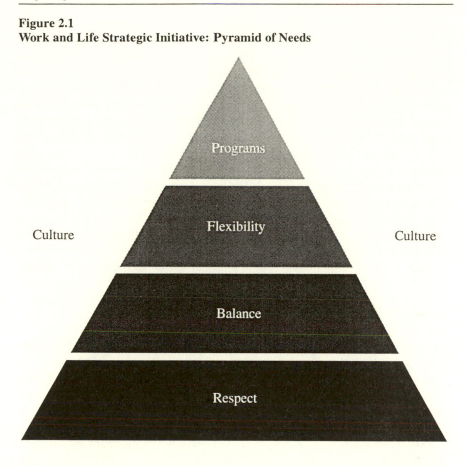

Culture   Culture

Culture

Source: The foregoing was published with permission from *The Work and Life Pyramid of Needs* by Alice Campbell of Baxter Healthcare Corporation and Marci Koblenz of MK Consultants. Copyright 1997 Baxter Healthcare Corporation and MK Consultants.

the understanding of the nature of work and life, enhances corporate strategic planning, and enables an organization to maximize its return on investment."[10]

In linking the two concepts, Campbell and Koblenz suggest that an effective work/life initiative will focus first on the pain workers feel related to the most basic needs (i.e., those rooted in respect for the dignity of the individual). Workers regard respect as an entitlement and not a benefit of working for a particular employer. Thus, the employer faces the highest level of risk in not addressing work and life conflicts related to respect for workers.

Like Maslow's theory, Campbell and Koblenz's paradigm describes a progressive process. In Maslow's theory, the individual will act first to satisfy the most basic needs before devoting energy and attention to fulfilling higher level needs. So, too, argue Campbell and Koblenz, the employer should not neglect the basic needs for respect, balance, and flexibility, and simply develop programs and policies to respond to categorical needs of employees. Failing to address basic needs puts the employer at greatest risk of negative outcomes. Therefore, to minimize risk, a work/life strategic initiative needs to focus on the "root" component(s), that is, the issue or issues that exist at the lowest of the four levels. For example, employer-sponsored activities related to balance, flexibility, and programs will be viewed as "lip service" by workers who feel that there is a general lack of respect for them as individuals in the work place.

Statements of such basic values as respect for the dignity of each person working in the organization need to be included in the organization's vision statement, which should paint a vivid picture of what an organization intends to become, and in its mission statement, which describes the organization's purpose in terms of its key constituencies. The "3-p" operational aspects of the work/family strategic initiative are important and highly visible. Programs like elder care resource and referral can deliver a high return on an employer's investment (see examples in Chapter 4). However, their successful implementation and acceptance rests upon the values of the organization.

Corporate culture is the environment within which all the other elements exist. There is a constant interaction among the organization's values, programs, policies, and practices and its corporate culture. Culture affects behavior and managerial practice and vice versa.

In the 1980s and early 1990s, many businesses embraced the necessity of implementing Total Quality Management (TQM) initiatives in order to remain competitive. At first, managers and workers clung to the traditional notion of quality assurance as an after-the-fact function assigned to a quality assurance department or staff person. The value of continuous quality improvement only gained full acceptance when top management committed their personal time and credibility as well as the organization's financial resources to retrain and reward workers for initiating change in practices throughout the organization. This required revamping financial and other reward systems. Ultimately, at some companies, it changed behavior, which in turn changed corporate culture. Until the marketplace demands that work/family balance is as important a competitive factor as implementation of TQM was in the early 1990s, organizations will realize only part of the potential benefits of implementing elder care–friendly programs, policies, and procedures.

Rosalind Barnett and Caryl Rivers suggest that one way a company can incorporate work/family concerns into the life of the organization is to develop and make use of a "family impact statement" as a way of doing business. "Just as some companies examine the impact of their acts on the environment before major decisions are made, managers would, as a matter of course, consider the impact of decisions and policies on the families of employees. Travel policies, meeting plans, job assignments, relocation plans, work hours, and leave and vacation policies would all be viewed in light of family impact. This won't mean that companies have to be turned upside down. In many cases, small changes can have major effects."[11]

A few employers are moving beyond the way of thinking that separates out work/family issues as something separate and distinct from day-to-day "business practices." For example, Bank Boston now includes several items relating to work/family behaviors as part of the eighteen-point annual evaluation process for all its management staff.

The manager who takes the time to examine individual and organizational readiness will have a firm foundation on which to begin the process of program planning to meet the needs of workers who are caring for older relatives. Chapter 3 focuses on understanding the needs of those working caregivers.

NOTES

1. Paula B. Doress-Worters and Diana Laskin Siegal, *The New Ourselves, Growing Older: Women Aging with Knowledge and Power* (New York: Simon & Schuster, 1994), 38.

2. Adapted from Erdman B. Palmore, *The Facts on Aging Quiz* (New York: Springer, 1998).

3. Leonard Hayflick, *How and Why We Age* (New York: Ballantine Books, 1994), 44.

4. Virginia Morris, *How to Care for Aging Parents* (New York: Workman Publishing, 1996), 15.

5. Martha Avery, "Prime Proposal," *New Directions for Women*, November–December 1984.

6. U.S. Bureau of the Census, "Family Disruption and Economic Hardship," *Current Population Reports*, series P-70, no. 23 (Washington, D.C.: U.S. Government Printing Office, 1991).

7. Renee Y. Magid and Melissa M. Codkind, *Work and Personal Life—Managing the Issues* (Menlo Park, Calif.: Crisp Publications, 1995), 51–52.

8. Julia Lawlor, "Bottom Line on Work–Family Programs," *Working Woman*, July 1996, 54.

9. Sally Coberly, *An Employer's Guide to Eldercare* (Washington, D.C.: Washington Business Group on Health, 1991), 45.

10. Alice Campbell and Marci Koblenz, *The Work and Life Pyramid of Needs: A New Paradigm for Understanding the Nature of Work and Life Conflicts* (Deerfield, Ill.: Baxter Healthcare and MK Consultants, 1997), 68–78.

11. Rosalind C. Barnett and Caryl Rivers, "Flex-ing It in the Workplace," *Boston Globe*, 21 May 1997, 27.

Chapter 3

Understanding the Needs of Working Caregivers

I'm in sales. Most of the time, I'm frazzled, nutty, working too many hours. . . . One night, after work, I drive down the Interstate like a maniac to this rehab place where my mother's living temporarily since she was discharged from the hospital. I walk into the lobby and everyone's moving in slow-mo. It's bizarre, a total culture shock after my eleven hour day handling calls on the cell phone and traveling from sales call to sales call. Invariably, the front desk is run by control freaks. They're used to ordering these poor old people around: "You got zee papers? You don't have zee papers? You got your number?" You really get a taste for what it's like to have no power. I made up my mind that I would do everything I could to get her back home and help her to stay there as long as she was able.
—Eileen, sales representative for a temporary staffing agency

Working caregivers come in many different shapes and sizes. Their situations include a broad spectrum of circumstances, from anticipatory caregiving, in which the adult child is not yet involved in direct care but may be assisting the elder with planning for future care needs, to full-time, hands-on personal care.

Across this care spectrum, caregiver needs fall into four broad categories:

1. *Time.* The flexibility to schedule work and caregiving activities in ways that allow for a balance between the two sets of responsibilities, and respite time, that is, time away from both work and caregiving, to allow for replenishment of energy.

2. *Timely Information.* Accurate, up-to-date information about services and resources will help lower caregiver stress while addressing the needs of the older person for whom care is being provided. The caregiver's challenge is to arrange the right help at the right place at the right time.

3. *Finances.* The ability to pay for care is a compelling issue for many caregivers. Meeting costs may require combining the financial resources of the elder, the working caregiver, other family members, and government or private sector programs.

4. *Emotional Support.* An understanding and caring attitude on the part of family members and coworkers—and perhaps the assistance of a professional counselor—can help sustain a working caregiver through stressful choices and tradeoffs.

This chapter begins with a description of the levels of intensity of caregiving experiences, highlighting the ways in which work-related adjustments vary according to these levels. The next section addresses what is known about working caregivers' needs for time, timely resources, finances, and emotional support, with emphasis on areas of special need that have particular relevance for program planning. The focus then changes to characteristics of working caregivers, listing some of the ways in which caregiving involvement varies by gender, ethnicity, age, and occupation. Finally, because more employers currently include child care than elder care as part of their work/life benefit packages, the chapter concludes with a comparison of these two types of dependent care, describing the five ways in which they differ.

LEVELS OF CAREGIVING INTENSITY

The demands on working caregivers and the corresponding levels of stress range from mildly distracting to mentally and physically exhausting. Individuals may have some fairly light responsibilities, such as making regular telephone calls to check on a relative's safety and well being. Others provide transportation, prepare occasional meals, or perform such household chores as yard work, cleaning, shopping, or laundry. Still other caregivers manage complex service arrangements, coordinating home care help or overseeing the elder's participation in a supervised program of care, perhaps adult day care, outside the home. Some live with the elder and are effectively on-call twenty-four hours a day for whatever need may arise.

The National Alliance for Caregiving (NAC) developed a level of care index for use in a national study which uses a statistically significant sample of all caregivers providing care for persons fifty years or older in the United States.[1] The study results profile the various impacts of family caregiving in today's society. The index categorizes caregivers into five levels of care, with level 1 being the lowest in caregiving demand or intensity and level 5 being the highest. Intensity of caregiving is measured according to the kinds and numbers of assistive activities the caregivers perform and the number of hours per week they devote to caring for their principal care recipients. Table 3.1 sum-

Table 3.1
Caregivers by Level of Care

	Percentage of All Caregivers	Mean Hours of Care Provided Per Week
Level 1	25.8	3.6
Level 2	13.8	8.2
Level 3	19.0	9.1
Level 4	23.5	27.3
Level 5	12.3	56.5
Missing	5.6	n.a.
Total	**100.0**	

Source: National Alliance for Caregiving (NAC) and the American Association of Retired Persons (AARP), *Family Caregiving in the U.S.: Findings from a National Survey* (Washington, D.C.: NAC and AARP, 1997).

marizes the findings regarding the percent of caregivers and the mean number of hours of care provided per week by level of care. Each successive level involves a higher degree of caregiving responsibility or demand. The mean number of hours of care per week provided by all caregivers is 17.9 hours.

Level 1 caregivers provide no assistance with personal care activities such as dressing or bathing the care recipient, and typically provide care for a maximum of eight hours per week. In contrast, level 5 caregivers assist with at least two personal care activities and provide care for more than forty hours per week.

There are important differences between those working caregivers who provide general elder care (most of whom fall into levels 1 and 2) and those who provide personal care (levels 3 through 5). As Table 3.1 shows, those who fall into the most intensive categories of caregiving (levels 4 and 5) experience far greater demands on their time than those in the less intensive categories. A majority (54.8%) of caregivers provide at least some personal care.

Neal, et al. point out that even working caregivers who are involved in less intensive levels of caregiving can experience job performance impact. "Simply anticipating . . . care can influence their choice of jobs, their readiness to take on more responsibility, and their willingness to consider geographic transfers."[2] However, as Table 3.2 shows, those who provide the most intensive levels of care (levels 3, 4, and 5) are far more likely to make work-related adjustments in order to continue to fulfill their caregiving responsibilities.

WORKING CAREGIVERS' NEEDS

Time

Janet has worked as an administrative assistant for the same utility company for ten years. Over the past two years, she has spent an increasing amount of time caring for her widowed mother who is partly paralyzed from a stroke. A neighbor checks in on her mother several times a day while Janet is at work. Other than that, Janet personally provides for all her mother's needs,

Table 3.2
Work-Related Adjustments by Level of Care

	Total	Level 1	Level 2	Level 3	Level 4	Level 5
Made any changes listed below	54.2	40.8	45.1	58.2	66.5	75
Changed daily schedule: go in late or leave early	49.4	36.3	44	54	61.5	64
Took leave of absence	10.9	5.5	5.9	9.1	17.8	26
Worked fewer hours or took less demanding job	7.3	2	3.8	6.5	11.7	25
Lost any job benefits	4.2	2.4	3.4	1.7	7.5	11
Turned down a promotion	3.1	1.2	2.1	0.7	6	10.4
Chose early retirement	3.6	1.2	0.3	3	5.1	14.8
Gave up work entirely	6.4	1.3	0.2	4.4	10.2	30.3

Source: National Alliance for Caregiving (NAC) and the American Association of Retired Persons (AARP), *Family Caregiving in the U.S.: Findings from a National Survey* (Washington, D.C.: NAC and AARP, 1997).

rising earlier in the morning to help dress, bathe, and feed her. Lately, her mother has become confused, and Janet fears leaving her alone in the suburban house they share.

Preoccupied with her mother's needs, Janet scoots home from work on her lunch hour to check on her mother personally and to feed her lunch. Janet loses time from work taking her mother to several doctor appointments, and she is constantly fatigued. She knows that the quality of her work, previously impeccable, is slipping as she struggles to maintain her mother at home. She cannot afford to pay someone to stay with her mother.

Janet is acutely aware of her failing ability to concentrate as she should on her job and feels anxious about work. She also feels guilty that she cannot "be there" for her mother to meet all her needs. Nearing the breaking point, Janet asks her supervisor if she can stagger her hours so she can have the flexibility of arriving or leaving when she needs to do so. Her request is flatly refused, and Janet quits her job.

Janet's story illustrates the kinds of needs and dilemmas faced by a person who wants to continue working productively while caring for a parent in failing health. Twenty-eight percent of nonworking caregivers say they left their jobs because they could not strike a balance between employment and caregiving responsibilities.[3] Each year, about 4 percent of all working caregivers who provide personal care, or about 229,000 American workers, quit or leave their work due to their responsibilities as caregivers.[4] In many cases, the inability to build in needed flexibility in terms of time creates an untenable situation.

Time is the number one need of working caregivers, with nearly half (49%) reporting having made changes in work schedule (going in late, leaving early, or taking time off during the day) to accommodate caregiving responsibilities. One in five caregivers say the biggest difficulty they face in providing care is the demand on their time or not being able to do what they want. Fulfilling commitments to older relatives requires substantial adjustments to free time, social activities, as well as timing and quality of care provided to the elder. In fact, caregivers say that the single most important form of help they could use is free time or a break from caregiving, with 17 percent of caregivers saying this is their highest priority need. Among those who provide many hours of personal care per week, 33 percent cite time as their number one need. Caregivers who are taking care of someone with dementia are also more likely (24%) than caregivers in general to cite time as their top need.[5]

What are the most common activities or kinds of assistance that require a commitment of time and money by working caregivers? The NAC study found that the most common types of help included four Instrumental Activities of Daily Living (IADLs):[6] assistance with transportation, grocery shopping, housework, and preparing meals. The three Activities of Daily Living (ADLs) include: getting in and out of chairs, dressing, and bathing. Tables 3.3 and 3.4 summarize the most common types of help provided by level of caregiving

Table 3.3
Performance of IADLs by All Caregivers and by Levels 1 and 5 (Percentages)

	Total	Level 1	Level 2
Transportation	79.3	72.0	89.5
Grocery Shopping	77.3	67.9	93.7
Housework	73.6	53.2	96.0
Preparing Meals	60.0	28.9	94.6
Managing Finances	55.6	48.3	74.4
Arranging or Supervising Outside Services	53.9	42.9	74.6
Giving Medicine	37.3	0.0	86.6
No ADLs	2.0	2.6	---

Source: National Alliance for Caregiving (NAC) and the American Association of Retired Persons (AARP), *Family Caregiving in the U.S.: Findings from a National Survey* (Washington, D.C.: NAC and AARP, 1997).

intensity. Table 3.4 includes only caregivers in levels 4 and 5, the highest levels of intensity of care, since these are the caregivers providing the most hands-on, personal care. An earlier study of caregivers at a large California-based company found that more than half of all the caregivers cited three types of service: companionship, transportation, and shopping assistance.[7] More than one-fourth of those caregivers were assisting with home maintenance, telephone calls, house cleaning, and financial management. Only about 8 percent were providing the kind of personal care that Janet provided for her mother (i.e., dressing, feeding, toileting).

In Janet's case, the ability to come into work later would have reduced her stress by allowing her to help her mother get up and dressed without the deadline pressure of an 8:30 A.M. work arrival time. The ability to take a midday break would have allowed her to prepare her mother's lunch without feeling guilty if she returned to the office in one hour and twenty minutes instead of the allotted one hour. With a lower stress level related to time pressures, Janet may well have coped and adapted more successfully.

Table 3.4
Service Provided by Long Distance Caregivers by Distance Away

Percentage who have helped with	Distance Away 1-2 hours	3+ hours
Advice and information	88	87
Transportation	76	51
Shopping	69	51
House and yard maintenance	57	51
Insurance forms, legal and financial	49	49
Meals	52	43
Housekeeping	55	38
Monthly expenses	31	37
Nursing care	41	29
Personal care (e.g., dressing, bathing)	33	29

Source: Donna L. Wagner, *Caring Across the Miles: Findings of a Study of Long-Distance Caregivers* (Washington, D.C.: National Council on the Aging, 1997), 22.

James, a product planner, had a similar experience to Janet's, but things turned out much better for him. Four years ago, James's eighty-six-year-old aunt had a stroke that left her unable to care for herself. James was the only relative available to help her. Though he had been close to his aunt most of his life, the caregiving role was something entirely new to him.

It took two months to find an acceptable nursing home for his aunt. The effort involved in locating a satisfying site required James to spend time visiting and evaluating several potential facilities. Thanks to his employer's flex-time approach, he was able to work half days during that time. James later arranged with his supervisor to work a flexible shift that typically starts at 6:30 A.M. This allows him to visit his aunt as she rises, to put in a full day of work, then to return to the nursing home on some evenings to chat with her before she goes to sleep for the night.

Timely Information

Peter, an association executive in New Jersey, became involved with the care of his seventy-year-old father when he was diagnosed with prostate cancer shortly after Peter's mother's death. Peter, who lived over an hour away from his father, became concerned when his father slipped into a deep depression. It was winter and the old boiler in his father's home was acting up; it required regular monitoring to ensure that an adequate amount of water remained in it. His father was not eating properly or sleeping well—partly because he worried that the boiler would break down in the middle of the night. In his depressed state, he felt constantly confused and could not perform everyday tasks.

To help his father get back on his feet, Peter, his sister Marilyn who lived nearby, and brother Pierre who lived four hours away, teamed up to provide the needed support. Through a network of personal and professional contacts in the health and social services fields, Peter took the lead in arranging needed care. Marilyn checked in on their father regularly and helped him with transportation when he needed it. Pierre called his father regularly, providing emotional support.

As their father's medical condition intensified, Peter coordinated the care provided by his father's primary care physician, his urologist, and, later, his oncologist. He also assisted him with bill-paying and arranged for a "friendly visitor" from a local agency to check in on him. Marilyn asked a friend to accompany their father to the daily lunchtime meal program at the senior center; she also helped with weekly food shopping. Peter scheduled the replacement of the old boiler and escorted his father on visits to assisted living residences and other alternative types of housing, so he could begin to see new options for his living situation.

All this took time. Peter's employer allowed him the flexibility to spend half a day per week visiting and assisting his father. He made up the time as needed by coming in earlier or working later. After about nine months, their father's depression began to lift and he regained control over many aspects of his day-to-day life. He sold the house and moved into an apartment in a relative's two-family home. Without the involvement of Peter, Marilyn, Pierre, and other family members and friends in researching, arranging, and assisting with follow-through of the many time-consuming details of a complex housing and services plan, Peter's father may very well have been placed in a nursing home. Peter's employer assisted greatly in giving him the time flexibility he needed. Peter and his siblings were accordingly able to help their father maximize his independence and self-reliance. Peter was subsequently able to taper off his involvement to visits on weekends once his father had settled into his new living situation.

Plethora of Agencies and Programs

In most major metropolitan areas of the United States, numerous agencies and programs offer an array of services and programs of assistance for elders. In broad terms, they fall into the categories of medical–health care (including mental health), housing, social services, financial assistance, recreation, transportation, nutrition, volunteer opportunities, and legal services.

The following partial list provides an overview of the kinds of services and resources that can be brought to bear in an elder caregiving situation.

Case management services
- Publicly funded elder care programs
- Managed care plans
- Private geriatric care managers

Financial information
- Social Security
- Supplemental Security Income (SSI)
- Food stamps
- Emergency funds
- Fuel assistance
- Financial planning and counseling

Health insurance information
- Medicare information
- Medicaid information (varies by state)
- Health Maintenance Organizations (HMOs) in Medicare and Medicaid
- Medicare supplemental health insurance
- Long-term care insurance
- Health insurance counseling services
- Claims assistance services

Health services
- Home health agencies
- Occupational therapy
- Physical therapy
- Adult day health care
- Geriatric physicians
- Geriatric assessment units
- Dental care
- Health screening programs
- Health-related equipment (durable medical equipment)
- Rehabilitation facilities
- Hospital services and programs
- Specialist physicians
- Hospice programs
- Nursing homes (subacute facilities, extended care facilities)

Home care services
- Homemaker agencies
- Personal care services
- Chore services
- Home repair
- Weatherization programs
- Emergency response systems
- Home security systems
- Telephone reassurance

Housing alternatives
- Assisted living residences
- Congregate housing
- Subsidized, low-income housing
- Shared housing
- Life care communities
- Foster care
- Emergency housing
- Home equity conversion
- Reverse annuity mortgage programs
- Property tax abatements
- Assistive technologies for the home

Legal services
- General advice and counsel
- Preparation of wills, estates, living trusts, and durable power of attorney
- Conservatorships and guardianships

Mental health services
- Counseling
- Caregiver support groups
- Social day care
- Crisis intervention
- Protective services and elder abuse programs

Nursing home related
- Listing of beds available, by level of care and ability to meet special needs
- Nursing home ombudsman programs
- State nursing home regulations
- Nursing home advocacy groups
- Counseling for nursing home placement
- Moving and house close-down services

Nutrition services

- Congregate dining
- Home delivered meals
- Food pantries
- Emergency food services
- Special diet meal programs
- Grocery delivery services
- Nutritional counseling

Social involvement and enhancement activities

- Senior centers
- Computer learning centers
- Volunteer programs (i.e., Retired Senior Volunteer Program)
- Employment placement and counseling services
- Educational opportunities
- Recreational opportunities (i.e., health clubs, YM and YWCAs)
- Senior citizens organizations
- Religious groups

Transportation

- Discounts on public transportation
- Specialized services (i.e., wheelchair-accessible van services)
- Vehicle conversions
- Subsidized medical transportation
- Volunteer-provided rides

The working caregiver must sort through all this information to find the right type of help, at the right time, in the right place, and at the right price. The more specialized services are not available in all areas, and the quality and cost of service may vary widely. Different nonprofit groups or government agencies at the state, county, or municipal level often impose income, age, and other eligibility requirements. Some of the more popular or basic programs have waiting lists. Once services are located and arranged, there are issues related to the ongoing quality of care.

The Six-Step Caregiving Process

The working caregiver faces a challenging, time-consuming six-step process in dealing with the elder services system.

First, the caregiver needs to collect accurate information about the elder's basic health condition, mental abilities, financial status, and housing situation, as well as social contacts and personal preferences. Once this base of information has been determined, the caregiver and elder can identify problem areas where a change in circumstances or the addition of services or resources would make an important difference in quality of life.

Second, the caregiver and the elder (to the extent that the elder is mentally capable) need to understand what types of services and resources are available in the community where the elder lives. This requires research, usually starting with the designated municipal and county agencies for elder affairs. In cases where the elder is mentally impaired, or otherwise incapable of collecting and sorting through such information, the caregiver must perform this function.

Third, the caregiver and elder need to be able to sort through those services which are available to determine which mix of service and at what cost makes the most sense in the elder's particular situation. This may involve the caregiver obtaining financial information to which family members have never before had access. A review of assets and liabilities may pose a source of some family conflict and may require objective, professional counsel.

Fourth, the caregiver and elder need to arrange for the required assistance. This involves contacting service providers and evaluating how the service can be made available when needed, at a cost the family can afford. Special conditions of the older person, such as mobility limitations, special diets, language barriers, and cultural preferences, may also have to be taken into consideration in selecting a service provider.

Fifth, the elder and the caregiver need to establish a way to monitor the quality of care. This will often involve ongoing communication with the service provider and perhaps, the elder's physician or case manager, in the case of older persons who are members of managed care plans. The purpose of maintaining contact with these professionals is threefold, to assure that (1) the elder is receiving neither more nor less care than is needed, (2) the service is delivered in accordance with professional standards and with courtesy and respect, and (3) someone is monitoring the elder's health status to identify important changes.

Sixth, both elder and caregiver need to adjust the care plan over time. Successfully adapting the housing, services, and social supports needed by the elder is a challenge and an art.

The elder service system is constantly changing. Printed materials summarizing the services available in a given locality are often soon out-of-date but are useful as a starting point in the service search. Information has also become available on the Internet, but the quality and reliability of the sources listed there varies widely.

There are elder care resource and referral vendors who specialize in serving the needs of working caregivers. These vendors maintain computerized databases of elder care resources and services. The best of these vendors update their files two or three times per week. Even a working caregiver who has access to such a continuously updated database of elder services needs strong skills in negotiating, record keeping, and diplomacy in order to develop and implement an effective plan of care.

Finances

The cost of long-term care for a disabled older relative is prohibitively expensive for some families. The average cost of a one-year stay in a nursing home is $40,000 and ranges as high as $80,000.[8] There is a 31-percent chance that a woman now sixty-five years old and a 14-percent chance that a man now sixty-five will spend a year or more in a nursing home.[9] And home care can cost as much or more than nursing home care. For example, sixteen-hours-per-day home care aide services, billed at $15.00 per hour, can cost a family $1,680 per week, which computes to $6,720 per month or $80,640 per year. The average cost of a single visit by a visiting nurse is $90.00.

A 1997 study found that only about half the respondents knew that people have to spend down all or almost all of their assets to get Medicaid benefits to pay for long-term care.[10] About one-third believe, incorrectly, that Medicare will pay for needed long-term care. Medicare does pay for most medical expenses incurred by older Americans, mainly doctor and hospital bills. Medicaid, the state–federal health care program which covers low income and disabled persons, pays the largest share (38%) of the nation's long-term care bill, with 43 percent of all long-term care paid for privately (see Figure 3.1).

A family may hope to combine public and private insurance programs to pay for long-term care needs, but, in reality, these programs usually pay only part of the cost of care, often leaving families financially strapped. Few older people have private long-term care insurance today, and the longer older people wait to purchase such coverage, the higher the premiums they must pay.

The number of working caregivers who cite financial hardship is relatively small. About 5 percent report this as a major problem, compared to 10 per-

Figure 3.1
Payment Sources, Long-Term Care

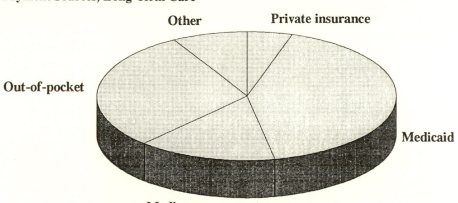

Source: Health Care Financing Administration, 1995.

cent of nonworking caregivers.[11] However, the proportion of working caregivers experiencing these difficulties is likely to rise. The reason for this is simple: the federal and state governments are tightening up eligibility for Medicaid-funded long-term care. Medicaid spending on long-term care for the elderly has been the fastest growing item in state budgets for a decade and policymakers are determined to rein in costs.

One of the strategies that states are pursuing in order to control Medicaid costs is to bring additional private resources into the long-term care system. This is accomplished in three ways: (1) by encouraging long term care insurance, (2) by moving aggressively to recover money from the estates of deceased Medicaid nursing home residents, and (3) by strictly enforcing prohibitions against transfer of assets prior to receiving long-term care. The latter strategy will put pressure on family caregivers to find the money to pay for long-term care from a combination of the elder's income and assets and other family resources. In support of this strategy, the U.S. Congress included a provision in the federal Balanced Budget Act of 1997 that holds attorneys criminally liable for providing advice or assistance to families seeking to shelter financial assets of older relatives from consideration in determining the elder's eligibility for Medicaid-covered long-term care.

The rapid growth (over 25% per year) in assisted living in the late 1990s illustrates the market-driven trend toward private funding of long-term care by elders and their families. Assisted living residences offer a new, more attractive alternative to placement in a traditional nursing home—and they operate almost entirely on a private pay basis. The goal of assisted living is to maximize the independent living potential for each older resident. The average assisted living residence charges $71.59 per day for a private room, or $28,000 per year, but the range is as much as $215.00 per day, or $78,000 per year. At least 20 percent of residents rely on family and other nongovernment sources of help to pay the bill.[12]

The financial issues related to elder caregiving are compounded by the fact that, for many older people, an open discussion of money matters is taboo. Caregivers walk a fine line between respecting the wishes of elders who do not want to divulge their financial situation and the desire to ensure elders' financial security. Elder care experts advise caregivers to tread lightly in this area and to avoid taking on too much responsibility for meeting elders' financial obligations.

The caregiver's self-interest and the interests of siblings also enter the picture. A caregiver who wants the best for a parent also may wish to preserve as much of the parent's assets so that they may be passed along to them upon the parent's death. When it comes to the management and disposition of parents' financial assets, the emotions of siblings can run high, and the closest of family relationships can be torn apart by financial issues. Even in situations where caregivers communicate clearly with siblings and handle financial matters openly, tensions can run high. For these reasons, involvement in the financial aspects of elder care can add substantially to the stress felt by working caregivers.

Emotional Support

As mentioned in the preceding paragraph, conflicts and misunderstandings about money can trigger powerful emotions in elders and in their family caregivers. Money issues are just one source of caregiver stress. Other major pressures include juggling many tasks into a limited amount of time, the physical strain of assisting some elders who require help getting in and out of bed or toilet transfers, and the fear of being reprimanded, or worse, by one's boss if one arrives late, leaves early, or misses too many days of work; add to this the interpersonal strains that accompany the change in roles between mother and daughter, father and son. Assuming new, often uncomfortable responsibilities for assisting elders with activities that they have always performed for themselves can also be an emotional strain. The statistics presented in Chapter 1 document the effects of emotional stress on working caregivers productivity and health condition. However, a manager can read the statistical reports without gaining empathy for the circumstances of working caregivers. Gaining a personal understanding of another person's specific experiences can help a manager grasp the reality of the stress they feel.

Lance, a professor at a West Coast university, took on the care of his Aunt Marie when she began to show signs of Alzheimer's disease at age seventy-five. Marie raised Lance when his parents died during his childhood. Over the years, Lance and his wife, Betty, had enjoyed a warm, cordial relationship with Marie as a next-door neighbor and as a close relative. Their children loved to visit and play with Aunt Marie after school. The first change Lance noticed was a marked shift in Marie's food preferences, but he did not think much of this. A month later, he came to visit at lunch time and found that she had not yet changed out of her pajamas. That had never been the case before. Soon after, their once articulate, fun-loving aunt began babbling incoherently every so often.

Lance and Betty convinced Marie to seek a diagnosis by a specialist who confirmed that she did, in fact, suffer from Alzheimer's disease. The disease progressed at an unusually rapid rate. Within a year and a half, she had become so agitated that she couldn't sit down. "She kept fidgeting all the time, taking her clothes off and putting them on. She lost most of her language. She had spoken English and Portuguese. Now, she spoke lots of Portuguese, but it was gibberish."

After two years, Marie fell and broke a hip, but with rehabilitation help, she relearned how to walk. "As the disease progressed, she became frailer and frailer," said Lance. "She spent the last ten months of her life screaming incessantly, at the top of her lungs, rolling on the floor. She was still at home at this point. She was incontinent. She had skin problems. . . . She had large open areas, very painful. Not the result of bad care, the body was simply not working, the skin was breaking down."

Lance convened a family meeting of Marie's two daughters and one son, all of whom lived within driving distance. They cooperated and shared in transporting her and handling household tasks. But Lance lived nearest and saw her most often.

"What was so hard was she would scream 'Help me!' at the top of her lungs every 20 seconds for maybe 20 hours a day. I mean blood-curling screams. At one point, I just couldn't take it any more, so I contacted her estranged husband of 20 years and convinced him that since they were not legally divorced, he was still financially responsible for her. He came and took care of her for the last seven months of her life."

Throughout the experience, Lance continued to fulfill his roles as husband, father, teacher, and researcher to the best of his ability. How did he cope? "I remember sometimes I would just go out on the back porch and scream myself," he said. "I'd go home, and if my wife was there, I'd say 'You go over there!' Somehow, we survived it."

In retrospect, Lance said his caregiving experience changed his view of his own aging. "I learned to live more for the day, for the moment. And not to say 'When I get older and retire, then I'll do this or that.' Instead, now I say 'Now's the time to do it, because you can't count on what your retirement years are going to be like.'"

Caregiving for elders with dementia can be very emotionally trying. Marie's case, in particular, took an extreme form. Lance's dedication and his ability to cope with a very high level of stress, however, is not unusual. When a manager encounters a caregiver in the safe, secure, relatively orderly environment of an office or plant, it may be impossible to fathom the intensity of the demands pressing on the worker from family responsibilities outside of work. Chapter 4 presents practical suggestions for early identification of the effects of caregiver stress and suggests ways a manager can behave that may enable caregivers to continue employment through times of emotional stress. Chapters 5 and 6 tell how to develop and implement responses that present options for working caregivers who might otherwise feel overwhelmed and trapped by their circumstances.

CHARACTERISTICS

Most of the literature describing working caregivers and caregiving focuses on the stresses felt by these individuals and the productivity losses felt by their employers. Managers need to recognize that the combination of elder caregiving and work can have positive effects as well. For the caregiver, continuing to work while caring for an elder can provide a respite from caregiving responsibilities, offer exposure to new resources, and enhance the caregiver's sense of self-confidence.[13] Elder caregiving, accordingly, may offer the caregiver rewards as well as stresses. A majority of caregivers interviewed for a recent study used positive words like "rewarded–rewarding," "happy," "helpful," "enjoyable," and "love–loving" to describe their caregiving experiences.[14]

Caregivers Do Not Self-Identify

Most adult children who are caring for ailing parents don't think of themselves as such, that is, they do not "self-identify" as caregivers. Rosalynn Carter mentions this phenomenon in her book on caregiving. She reflects on the fact that, even though she had become involved in the care of her seriously ill father at the age of twelve, "I never realized that I too was a caregiver until I became involved with the Rosalynn Carter Institute's caregiving program" after her years as first lady.[15]

Beth, a writer who lives in California, put it this way: "I never knew the term caregiver until six months after my parents passed away. They died five weeks apart, 2,000 miles from me, after almost two years of agonizing deterioration. The role of caregiver is such that there isn't usually time to think about it; there is too often only heartache, crisis, and need. By the end of the first year of my caregiving experience, I was barely able to drag myself along the commute to work, 50 miles each way. There was no rest at home, either. . . . I had no ability to concentrate or to remember, worrying about how to pay for more trips home, how to keep my parents together. I was apathetic, depressed. My waking moments were singed with anguish, my nights gasping for breath, gnashing my teeth and screaming. I had arrhythmia and chronic exhaustion. Foolishly, I never dared ask for time off."[16]

Because caregivers often will not identify themselves as such and probably will not share dilemmas in a social setting at work, managers may only learn of their predicaments through observing changes in behavior related to the stresses they are feeling. For this reason, it is important for management to provide information on an ongoing basis, to reach caregivers before their burdens grow to the point where stress is interfering with job performance.

Distractions at work, a diminished ability to concentrate and remember things, or an unusual pattern of tardiness or absences from work can all indicate an underlying elder care crisis in workers' situations. An employer can help many workers avert "caregiver crisis" by using the channels of communication within the organization to provide simple, useful information that caregivers can use as they take on new responsibilities. Chapter 5 provides specific communication techniques and messages to address this issue.

Women, Men, and Caregiving

Female caregivers not only outnumber males by a ratio of nearly three to one (see Figure 1.1), they also provide more hours of care per week than male working caregivers. Women are overrepresented among those caregivers providing "constant" (i.e., 40 hour per week) care: While women represent 73 percent of all caregivers, they constitute 79 percent of constant caregivers.

There are important differences in the way working men and women cope with elder caregiving responsibilities. Studies have shown that, on the average, male caregivers are less likely than female caregivers to provide domestic (e.g., house cleaning) and personal care services, while such tasks as decision making, financial management, and providing linkages to outside resources are equally provided by men and women.[17] Female working caregivers are also more likely than males to change their work schedules to accommodate their caregiving responsibilities.

Female caregivers also experience considerably higher stress than do male caregivers. Women are more likely than men to have experienced physical or mental problems as a result of caregiving.[18] Reasons for this may include the fact that male caregivers tend to obtain more help from others and that men and women tend to deal with their responsibilities in different ways.[19] For example, caregiving husbands may be more likely than caregiving wives to carve out personal time away from their impaired spouses. Other research shows that female caregivers tend to conceive of caregiving as a reflection of self-worth, that is, adult daughters feel that their mothers' continued requests for assistance indicate that they have failed as caregivers.[20]

An increasing number of men are becoming involved in the care of older relatives. The aging of the population is one factor influencing this role shift; there are more frail older people than ever before, so more men are becoming aware of their needs. In addition, the increase in two wage-earner households and the movement of more women into the ranks of management and professional leadership has created a host of new issues for couples. For example, if a husband's work load is lighter or if his employer allows for more scheduling flexibility, he may take the lead in organizing needed care, allowing the wife to focus more of her energy on the job.

Ethnicity and Caregiving

Cultural traditions can influence the amount and types of care provided by working caregivers from different ethnic backgrounds. Yet, few large-scale surveys (with the one notable exception cited below) have examined the differences among caregivers by ethnic group, and even fewer have specifically looked at the circumstances of working caregivers from different ethnic backgrounds. One study found that nonwhites were less likely to alter their work backgrounds than their white working caregiver counterparts.[21] Neal et al. speculate that this difference may relate to the fact that nonwhites may be more likely to work jobs that offer fewer options for job schedule flexibility than whites.

The National Alliance for Caregiving survey addressed caregiving issues across four racial–ethnic groups in the United States: whites, blacks, Hispanics, and Asians.[22] A sampling of significant differences reported in that survey includes the following:

- Asian and Hispanic caregivers are significantly younger than whites and are more evenly split among male and female caregivers; 52 percent are female, compared to 77 percent of blacks, 74 percent of whites, and 67 percent of Hispanics. In addition, Asian caregivers report higher annual incomes than other groups. The authors speculate that this may be due to the fact that more recent Asian immigrants (with lower incomes) were excluded from the survey, which sampled English-speaking caregivers only.
- Black, Hispanic, and Asian caregivers more often live in households that also include children under the age of eighteen.
- Black caregivers are more likely than other groups to be caring for a relative other than an immediate family member or grandparent.
- White caregivers tend to care for persons who are older than those cared for by caregivers of other racial–ethnic groups, with a mean age of 77.6, compared to 75.2 for blacks, 74.7 for Hispanics, and 74.4 for Asians.
- Asian caregivers are more likely to live in the same household with their care recipient, but they are also least likely to be caring for a person over eighty-five years old. About 15 percent of Asians care for the "old-old," compared to 25 percent among whites and 24 percent among blacks.
- Blacks and Hispanics more frequently reported financial hardship in caregiving than whites or Asians. However, nonworking caregivers in general were more likely to find caregiving a financial hardship than working caregivers (10% versus 5%).

Age, Occupation, and Caregiving

Issues related to balancing work and family caregiving are not felt exclusively by older workers. Evidence is inconclusive as to whether there is a correlation between increased stress and the working caregivers' chronological age. Some studies suggest older workers feel more stress related to caregiving. However, at least one study found increased absenteeism among caregivers who were female, younger, and caring for a spouse or parent.[23] These younger caregivers tended to miss more work and found it more difficult to balance work and family issues, perhaps in part because of a lack of internal synchronization with their "social clocks."

Gerontologist Bernice Neugarten's concept of a social clock suggests that the experience of caring for an older relative may be more "on-time" and hence a more "normal" experience for older people (i.e., those forty and older) than for younger people.[24] Accordingly, the younger worker who must deal with elder care issues may find the experience more inherently stressful than an older worker. Though the largest group of caregivers is comprised of those between the ages of thirty-five and forty-nine, more than one in five caregivers (22%) are under the age of thirty-five (see Figure 1.2).

One's occupation also affects the range of options available for coping with the demands of elder care and work. Stone and others have shown that workers in clerical, sales, professional, and managerial positions are more likely to rearrange their work schedules to accommodate elder care responsibilities than workers in blue collar jobs. Blue collar workers were more likely to accommodate caregiving needs by taking time off without pay.[25] Neal et al. report on another study which compared the experiences of two different groups of caregivers: care managers (those who arrange for services for care recipients), and care providers (those who directly provide personal care). The study found that among the working caregivers, "The care managers tended to have higher status jobs and higher incomes than the care providers. The higher job status allowed the former group more flexibility to fulfill their caregiving responsibilities than did those of the latter group. Further, due to the importance of their more socially valued jobs, the care managers also experienced less conflict about continuing to work than did the care providers and more ease in delegating caregiving responsibilities. The care providers, whose jobs were less valued and provided them with less income, sometimes quit work to become full-time caregivers."[26]

Long Distance Caregiving

A growing number of American workers who have elder care responsibility are attempting to fulfill their duties on a long-distance basis. In these situations, the caregiver and care recipient do not live in physical proximity to one another.

In the fall of 1996, the National Council on the Aging undertook the first national study of long distance caregivers and defined a long distance caregiver as one who resides more than a one-hour automobile drive from the care recipient.[27] Wagner, who authored the study, estimated that there were about 4.8 million long distance *working* caregivers in the United States, representing 72 percent of the 6.7 million total number of long distance caregivers. Ninety percent of them (4.3 million) work full time. The study also revealed the following:

- The caregivers live, on average, about three hundred miles from the persons they help, with an average travel time of about four hours. About one-fourth live more than four hundred miles or six or more hours away.

- Long distance caregiving is a family affair. About half of long distance caregivers are not the primary caregiver, but have helped others take care of the older person. Another 31 percent say they share the responsibility equally with others. Regardless of how far away they live, a high proportion of long distance caregivers provide advice, information, and emotional support to the care recipient.

- Those who live three or more hours away are less likely to provide help with such tasks as transportation, shopping, and house and yard maintenance (see Table 3.4), but are more likely to help out with the care recipient's monthly expenses.

Family, friends, and volunteers (especially from religious organizations with which the care recipient is affiliated) play an important role in supplementing the care provided by long distance caregivers.

Those who serve as primary caregivers are much more likely than those who have taken on less caregiving responsibility to help with legal and financial matters and to help pay monthly expenses.

Only about 20 percent of long distance caregivers provide direct cash assistance, providing an average of $202.00 per month on direct cash subsidy. However, the average long distance caregiver does spend about $196.00 per month on caregiving-related expenses (including travel and telephone expenses).

Long distance caregiving is stressful. More than one-third describe their primary role as providing emotional support. Fully two-thirds of caregivers in these circumstances feel at least some stress related to their responsibilities. About half say that caregiving responsibilities interfere with their personal, social, and family needs. They report that the two biggest sources of stress are the distance between themselves and the care recipient and accepting and dealing with the condition of the care recipient. One in seven reports worsening health due to caregiving responsibilities. Persons who report caregiving to be stressful are more likely to be caring for a male or for a person with behavioral problems.

Over 40 percent of long distance caregivers report some difficulty in finding care arrangements for the persons they are helping. Yet, working long distance caregivers reported only minimal effects on work. For example, interruptions at work due to caregiving-related phone calls is experienced by about 40 percent of long distance caregivers, but more intense work disruptions are less common (i.e., missing entire days of work [25%] or making adjustments in regular work hours [20%]). Those who live three or more hours away from the care recipient are more likely than those living closer to say they typically miss at least one day of work because of caregiving.

How Long Distance Caregivers Differ from Other Caregivers

• Long distance caregivers have substantially higher average annual incomes ($55,029) than caregivers in general ($35,000), though their income levels are comparable to household incomes for the age group forty-five to fifty-four nationwide who have a median income of $55,029.

• The gender breakdown among long distance caregivers is quite different:

	Long Distance Caregivers	Caregivers Overall
Men	46 percent	28 percent
Women	54 percent	72 percent

Like other caregivers, those who are caring for some one on a long distance basis need timely, accurate information and advice, though a substantial number of these caregivers do not seek advice from anyone (see Table 3.5).

Almost half of long distance caregivers are able to use the Internet, and most are very receptive to using this method of obtaining information to assist them in their caregiving responsibilities.

Table 3.5
Top Ten Sources of Information and Advice for Long Distance Caregivers

Source	Percentage
Family Members	37
No one	28
Recipient's Physician	19
Friends	11
Local aging offices or Area Agencies on Aging	7
Clergy	6
Nursing home staff	6
Social worker	5
Hospital staff	5

Source: Donna L. Wagner, *Caring Across the Miles: Findings of a Study of Long-Distance Caregivers* (Washington, D.C.: National Council on the Aging, 1997), 44.

The unmet need expressed most frequently by long distance caregivers is the inability to spend more time with the care recipient because they live at a distance. Emotional concerns (e.g., their inability to cope with the person's illness or not getting cooperation from the care recipient) are also high on the list (see Table 3.6).

Long distance caregivers say they would find it helpful to have access to training and educational materials about aging and services for older people. Another type of help they say they can use: visits to the care recipient by a volunteer from a religious organization who would both help with daily activities and provide updates to the caregiver on the person's condition. About half of the long distance caregivers responding to the Wagner study say it would be helpful to have a support group composed of other caregivers.[28]

Table 3.6
Top Ten Unmet Needs of Long Distance Caregivers

Greatest unmet need of caregiver in terms of helping the person	Percentage
Physical Concerns	34
Inability to spend time or live at a distance	25
None	16
Emotional concerns	14
Financial concerns	11
Money or financial means to help more or to secure better living conditions	9
Having sufficient information to make knowledgable decisions	6
Provide assisted living or personal care	6

Source: Donna L. Wagner, *Caring Across the Miles: Findings of a Study of Long-Distance Caregivers* (Washington, D.C.: National Council on the Aging, 1997), 46.

Among those long distance caregivers who could name a particular service that they would like to purchase, the top three services listed are the following: (1) assisted living or help with personal care, (2) nursing care or full-time care, and (3) companion and home health aide services. However, most respondents (30%) to this question said they did not know which service or services they would most like to purchase, indicating a need for better information about options and the care that is available.

The Number of Long Distance Caregivers Is Growing

When the AARP did a national study of caregivers in 1987, they estimated that the total number of caregivers in the United States was 7 million. In 1997, the NAC study estimated that there were 7 million long distance caregivers among a total of over 25 million family caregivers in the United States.[29] Based on this information, it is safe to say that the number of long distance caregivers in the United States has grown substantially in recent years. The continuing trend toward corporate consolidations, mergers, and acquisitions, and the related relocation of offices and facilities has often required workers to move or lose their jobs. Given these demographic and economic trends, it is safe to say that the number of long distance caregivers will continue to increase in the future.

HOW ELDER CARE AND CHILD CARE DIFFER

A professional in Virginia compared the level of difficulty between long distance caregiving for his father with his experiences with child-rearing: "For one thing, you're not dealing with a dependent. You don't have the authority, necessarily, to intervene. You need to add to that sibling disputes over who should help and how. You call state agencies and you get a recording. Or someone's not helpful. Or it's the wrong number. . . . This is probably the hardest thing a family can go through. It defies the complexity of what people go through with children."

Caring for a child who is not disabled or chronically ill typically follows predictable patterns or stages. For example, newborn care means sleepless nights. The toddler stage includes the search for quality, affordable day care, and coping with common early childhood illnesses. When a son or daughter enters grammar school, the entire family makes new adjustments. This is also true with the transition to adolescence, high school, and entering college. These important, sometimes stressful life events require certain coping skills and services. Elder care is an entirely different matter.

Adult-to-Adult Relationship

Most important, elder care involves one adult caring for another adult. When little Johnny does not feel like going to school in the morning, Mom or Dad can simply tell him that he will go to school, escort him to the school door, and drop him off there. In some instances, the adult must exercise decision making for the child in the child's best interest. This is not the case in an elder care situation.

No matter how debilitated, the elder is an adult, and as such, has the right to make choices about how and where to live, to the extent of course that the elder is responsibly able to make such decisions. The elder's right to self-determination can often conflict with the working caregiver's perception of what is proper, safe, or appropriate care. Conflict may also ensue when the elder's decisions inconvenience the adult child or vice versa. In a healthy caregiving relationship, the adult son or daughter respects the autonomy and decision-making capacity of the elder.

Coping with elder care is further complicated by the history of relationships between parents and children and among siblings. Situations where parents and adult children are estranged from one another or where there is a history of difficult and hurtful relationships add stress for all concerned.

In addition to the underlying reality of an adult-to-adult relationship, elder care differs from child care in four important ways: (1) There is greater variability and unpredictability; (2) there exists the need to arrange assistance from a variety of professionals and agencies, as well as relatives, friends, and neighbors; (3) long-term involvement is often required; and (4) the possibility of long distance caregiving exists.

Greater Variability and Unpredictability

Each individual ages at his or her own rate. While a ninety year old may live a healthy, independent lifestyle, requiring little help from others, a sixty-two-year-old parent with emphysema may need daily health monitoring and a significant amount of day-to-day help with such activities of daily living as cleaning the house, grocery shopping, and meal preparation. Different diseases progress differently and require varied kinds of self-care, professional oversight, and intervention. Other factors include the housing and financial situation of the elder, and the family and interpersonal dynamics within the family.

Complex Care Arrangements

Arranging care that matches elders needs and helps elders maintain their highest feasible level of decision-making and independence requires knowledge of the elder service system, the skills to negotiate that system successfully, and the time to work with the elder to put the pieces together. For most caregivers, this means either devoting an enormous amount of time to learn the system or engaging a care manager who acts as a surrogate family member to perform these tasks for them on behalf of the ailing parent.

Long-Term Care Can Mean Long-Term Involvement

The third way in which elder care differs from child care is that it often involves long-term care and long-term involvement. The average duration of an elder caregiving experience is four-and-one-half years.[30] As pointed out in Chapters 1 and 2, the need for elder care is often rooted in the presence of one or more chronic illnesses. Unlike a broken leg or a bad cold that might lay up a younger person for a few days or weeks, long-term illnesses can constrict the activities of older people for months or years. Some chronic conditions, like arthritis, can take a slow, steady toll, gradually reducing the ability of the elder to cook, clean, and dress him or herself. Others, like diabetes, may be successfully kept in check through conscientious self-management of the condition. However, if needed precautions are not taken, such situations can result in acute medical problems, falls, and other injuries that lead to hospitalizations and nursing home placements. Working with elders to adapt to

changing capabilities while maintaining autonomy and maximum independent functioning can sometimes require long term involvement.

The four key elements involved in successfully managing a long-term care
situation may be visualized as the legs of a four-legged stool. In order for elders
to navigate the many changes and challenges of chronic illness, they need access
to (1) adequate financial resources, (2) appropriate housing, (3) quality medical
and social services, and (4) timely and accurate information about all of the above.

Very often, the working caregiver whose parent is suffering from the effects of a chronic illness finds that the parent has done little or no planning in
relation to any of the four legs of the long-term care stool. As a result, the
working caregiver, the aging relative, and the entire family experience the
situation as a crisis. Perhaps the mother has suddenly been hospitalized and
cannot return home safely without ongoing assistance with many tasks that
she had always performed on her own. Suddenly, the adult child is faced with
questions like the following:

- Does Mother have adequate health insurance coverage to pay for ongoing home
  care help? She most probably does not, since only about 1 percent of elders have
  policies that cover long-term care.
- Is Mother's home safe and accessible in her impaired condition? For example, can
  she still navigate a flight of stairs? Are the kitchen and bathroom free of barriers
  and hazards which could result in injury-producing falls?
- Does one physician have the overview of Mother's health, or has she been dealing
  with a series of specialists, each focusing on one facet of her medical condition?
  How many different medications is she taking? Is she conscientious about taking
  the proper dosages at the proper intervals? Does she have a significant impairment
  in memory or mental acuity?
- Where can Mother turn if she needs help with shopping assistance or transportation
  to medical appointments? Is she eating properly?

A host of issues require attention—issues never before faced by most families. The caregiver needs to work with the parent and other family members
to both cope with the immediate situation and to anticipate the parent's future
needs by developing a plan that addresses the financial, housing, service, and
information dimensions of the situation.

Long Distance Caregiving

Parents and their children generally live in the same household. This is not the
case with elders and their adult children. In 80 percent of elder care relationships,
the caregiver and the care recipient maintain separate residences. In most instances where the elder and the caregiver do live together, they began doing so
because of the care recipient's need for care.[31] The section entitled "Caregiver
Characteristics" mentioned earlier in this chapter provides additional information about the phenomenon of long distance caregiving.

EFFECTIVE CAREGIVING

Good intentions not withstanding, many people are not cut out to be effective caregivers. In their book on caring for aging parents, Cohen and Eisdorfer liken the skills needed to effectively care for an elder to those needed in managing a family business: "Tasks like managing the financial aspects of care, coordinating the people directly and indirectly involved, mobilizing technical and professional support, and finding housing and transportation are also tasks done by managers and executives in business. What does the business world tell us about a successful manager? What qualities make an effective person? If you are an effective person,

- You know yourself.
- You are aware of the impact you have on other people.
- You can accept weaknesses.
- You can identify strengths in others.
- You can accept others who are different from you or who think differently from how you do.
- You have a flexible style.
- You create a trusting environment for people to think, work, and live in.
- You can manage conflict."

Cohen and Eisdorfer advise that caregivers assess their capabilities in relation to this list. They recommend that caregivers who do not see these characteristics in themselves should reach out to other members of the family to play a leadership role in managing care.[32] Sometimes, there is no other appropriate family member who is willing or able to do this. In such cases, the family needs to engage help from a professional, such as a private geriatric care manager.

Chapter 4 explores the ways in which a manager can identify working caregivers and encourage them to maximize their effectiveness in balancing their work and family responsibilities. Chapters 5 and 6 describe specific policies, procedures, and programs that can help caregivers address the needs we have examined in this chapter.

NOTES

1. National Alliance for Caregiving (NAC) and the American Association of Retired Persons (AARP), *Family Caregiving in the U.S.: Findings from a National Survey* (Washington, D.C.: NAC and AARP, 1997), 26.

2. Margaret B. Neal, Nancy J. Chapman, Berit Ingersoll-Dayton, and Arthur C. Emlen, *Balancing Work and Caregiving for Children, Adults, and Elders* (Newbury Park, Calif.: Sage Publications, 1993), 114.

3. Andrew E. Scharlach and Sandra Boyd, "Caregiving and Employment: Results of an Employee Survey," *The Gerontologist* 29, no. 3 (1989): 382.

4. Metropolitan Life Insurance Company, *The MetLife Study of Employer Costs for Working Caregivers* (Westport, Conn.: MetLife, 1997), 3.

5. NAC and AARP, *Family Caregiving*, 31.

6. An Instrumental Activity of Daily Living (IADL) is an activity performed to manage one's daily life or maintain a household and live independently, such as preparing a meal, grocery shopping, driving or using transportation systems, doing light housework, taking medications, managing finances and paying bills, or using the telephone.

7. Scharlach and Boyd, *Caregiving and Employment*, 382.

8. "Reducing Medicaid Spending on Long Term Care," *Policy and Research Report* (Summer–Fall 1996): 12.

9. Matthew Greenwald and Associates, *The John Hancock/NCOA Long Term Care Survey—Initial Findings* (Washington, D.C.: National Council on the Aging, 1997), 6.

10. Greenwald and Associates, *The John Hancock/NCOA Survey*, 6–7.

11. NAC and AARP, *Family Caregiving*, 24.

12. The Assisted Living Federation of America (ALFA), *The Assisted Living Industry—1996* (Fairfax, Va.: ALFA, 1997), 15.

13. Neal et al., *Balancing Work and Caregiving*, 129.

14. NAC and AARP, *Family Caregiving*, 26.

15. Rosalynn Carter with Susan K. Golant, *Helping Yourself Help Others: A Book for Caregivers* (New York: Times Books, 1994), 22.

16. Beth Witrogen McLeod, "A Self-Portrait of a Caregiver and Her Parents," *Take Care! National Family Caregivers Association Newsletter* (Fall 1996): 1–8.

17. Neal et al., *Balancing Work and Caregiving*, 116.

18. NAC and AARP, *Family Caregiving*, 23.

19. B. Miller, "Gender and Control among Spouses of the Cognitively Impaired: A Research Note," *The Gerontologist* 27 (1987): 447–453.

20. E. K. Abel, "Family Care of the Frail Elderly," *Circles of Care: Work and Identity in Women's Lives* (1990): 65–91.

21. R. I. Stone and P. F. Short, "The Competing Demands of Employment and Informal Caregiving to Disabled Elders," *Medical Care* 28 (1990): 513–526.

22. NAC and AARP, *Family Caregiving*, 8–23.

23. Neal et al., *Balancing Work and Caregiving*, 133.

24. B. L. Neugarten, ed., "Adult Pesonality: Toward a Psychology of the Life Cycle," *Middle Age and Aging: A Reader in Social Psychology* (Chicago: University of Chicago Press, 1968), 137–147.

25. Neal et al., *Balancing Work and Caregiving*, 118–119, 135.

26. Neal et al., *Balancing Work and Caregiving*, 119.

27. Donna L. Wagner, *Caring Across the Miles: Findings of a Study of Long-Distance Caregivers* (Washington, D.C.: National Council on the Aging, 1997), 11.

28. Wagner, *Caring Across the Miles*, 48.

29. NAC and AARP, *Family Caregiving*.

30. NAC and AARP, *Family Caregiving*, 12.

31. NAC and AARP, *Family Caregiving*, 15.

32. Donna Cohen and Carl Eisdorfer, *Caring for Your Aging Parents* (New York: G. P. Putnam's Sons, 1993), 105.

Chapter 4

The Individual Manager's Response

When people feel they're being supported in the work place, when they feel
that they are being seen as people with lives outside the work place, they
appreciate it. And that translates into commitment to the organization.
                                                                    —Barbara Wolf,
               Director, Office of Work and Family, Harvard University

Two assumptions underlie the recommendations in the next two chapters: (1)
the manager and the organization for which the manager works both value
their workers and (2) the manager wishes to address elder care issues in the
most cost effective manner possible.

This chapter focuses on responses to elder care issues in the work place on
the individual level. A review of four basics of good management serves as
the starting point for developing effective responses to elder care needs. Since
conflict is at the heart of work/family situations, the approach described here
provides the manager with the tools needed to assure that the inevitable conflicts encountered at work can be positive ones. Common dilemmas are explored, along with a four-step process for dealing effectively with elder care
issues of subordinates or peers.

Chapter 5 will then present a step-by-step process for dealing with elder care
on the organizational level in terms of policies, practices, and benefits—including specific ways to measure the cost effectiveness of elder care initiatives.

ASSUMPTIONS

The two assumptions accordingly provide the framework for action. The first is that the leaders of the organization value the people working within it.

Valuing the People in the Organization

When an organization values its people, feelings of trust among workers run high. An investment in creating and maintaining trust among workers heightens the organization's image and pays dividends in loyalty, commitment, and productivity.

In today's economy, every business is a service business, and in the words of Mike Vance, creative problem-solving consultant to some of the world's most successful firms, "If you want to provide excellent service to your customers, develop excellent working relationships among your people." One way to develop those excellent working relationships is to recognize that workers have a life outside of work. People appreciate their manager's understanding this simple fact. Workers do not necessarily expect their employer to solve their problems, but they do appreciate being given flexibility when they need it.

The Goal Is to Address Elder Care Issues as Cost Effectively as Possible

When does a program intended to help workers balance work and family responsibilities make business sense? Where does a manager draw the line? What is the return on the organization's investment in working caregivers? It is possible to measure the impact of elder care programs, and it is important to do so.

The examples that follow assume, for simplicity, that the manager is the primary person to whom the working caregiver can turn for help. That is, the organization has neither a human resources staff specialist to provide advice, nor an elder care consultation and referral service, nor an Employee Assistance Program capable of handling elder care needs.

Trust among coworkers is the key to identifying elder care issues earlier and avoiding lost time, reduced productivity, and as many conflicts as possible. The manager can build trust and minimize conflicts by exercising basic skills of good management.

TRUST: CHECKING THE BALANCE IN THE EMOTIONAL BANK ACCOUNT

Caregiving issues can be emotionally charged. Dealing effectively with them requires managers to establish and maintain a basic level of trust between themselves and each of the people with whom they work—because an elder care crisis can erupt at any time.

Trust does not materialize out of thin air; it develops over time. Stephen R. Covey coined the term "Emotional Bank Account" as a way to think about and measure the trust level in relationships among coworkers and others. "We all know what a financial bank account is. We make deposits into it and build up a reserve from which we can take withdrawals when we need to. An Emotional Bank Account is a metaphor that describes the amount of trust that's been built up in a relationship. It's the feeling of safeness you have with another human being."[1]

If a caregiver feels safe discussing his or her situation with the manager to whom he or she reports, then the chances are good that manager and worker can achieve a common understanding of the problem—a basic step toward finding workable solutions. "If I make deposits into an Emotional Bank Account with you through courtesy, kindness, honesty, openness, and keeping commitments to you, I build up a reserve. Your trust toward me becomes higher, and I can call upon that trust many times if I need to. I can even make mistakes and that trust level, that emotional reserve, will compensate for it. My communication may not be clear, but you'll get my meaning anyway. You won't make me an 'offender for a word.' When the trust account is high, communication is easier, instant, and effective."[2] When a large proportion of workers in an organization feel they have a "positive balance" in their individual Emotional Bank Accounts, the result is a climate in which loyalty can thrive. Loyalty is one manifestation of positive morale, which in turn translates into workers' willingness to go the extra mile to meet or exceed job expectations.

GOOD MANAGEMENT BASICS

Managing elder care conflicts well is a subset of managing people well. To succeed, a manager needs to pay consistent attention to four elements of good management: (1) clear accountability for performance; (2) open, honest, and ongoing communication; (3) job design flexibility; and (4) respect for privacy and confidentiality. Each of these elements is described in the following sections.

Accountability

Clear accountability for fulfilling responsibilities is a key factor that must be in place if the parties are to deal effectively with work/family conflicts like elder care. A clearly written, up-to-date job description and mutually agreed upon goals are a necessary starting point, a base for common understanding to which worker and supervisor can refer in the course of working together. Once the job description and goals are set, it is critical that individuals know what level of authority they have to accomplish their responsibilities. Trust can be diminished when authority for the same accountability varies among coworkers.

The manager needs to assure that these basic building blocks of clear communication are in place before work/family conflicts arise. Specific tasks include:

- Updating job descriptions at least annually.
- Setting specific, quantifiable goals for the individual, department, or team.
- Involving team members in a regular review and discussion of progress toward goals, at least once every three months.
- Conducting open and honest performance evaluations at least annually.

Open and Honest Communication

Smooth day-to-day operations require honesty and openness between managers and workers. Yet, they are not widely practiced in the work place. Richard Hamermesh of the Center for Executive Development has found that "Even the most powerful executives—people who readily make speeches in rooms full of investment analysts, who testify before Congress, who are able to issue orders that result in thousands of layoffs—cringe at the thought of sitting down with a subordinate to discuss a performance issue."

"Speaking the truth has two components: honesty and openness. There is a subtle difference between the two. To be honest means that there can be no posturing and no careful selection of words. Discussions are candid. To be open means that all issues can be raised. A company needs both forms of telling the truth."[3]

The answers to the following questions can reflect the type of communication that exists in the organization:

How approachable are managers in the organization?

Do managers get surprises that they shouldn't be getting?

Are people rewarded for giving negative as well as positive feedback?

Are problems actively elicited or allowed to grow until they become too costly or complex to ignore (or resolve)?

Do managers share their problems with others?

Do managers identify areas where they need to work with others?

Do managers feel comfortable asking for help?

Flexibility

A sure-fire way to guarantee repeated crises related to work/family conflicts and to assure unnecessary, costly turnover is to keep workers isolated from one another, provide little or no information about coworkers' responsibilities and priorities, and insist that each individual unwaveringly adhere to a prescribed set of specific tasks that no one else fully understands. Restated in positive terms: A manager can save himself or herself a lot of headaches by paying attention to designing jobs with flexibility in mind.

Some managers think that allowing for flextime or job sharing implies weak organizational structure and a lack of standards in managing worker performance. This could not be further from the truth. In fact, allowing for creativity in how a group of workers fulfills responsibilities requires better organization and clearer standards than the look-over-your-shoulder brand of supervision. The manager needs to pay attention to the following:

- Cross-training people, so they can fill in for each other in a pinch.
- Continually developing intellectual (planning), emotional (honesty), interpersonal (listening), and, when appropriate, managerial (delegating) behaviors.
- Assuring a continuing flow of need-to-know information among workers, including regular updates on the "big picture," so they understand how what they do contributes to where the organization is headed.
- Supporting a team approach to problem sensing and solving and achieving goals.

People are not born with team management skills. They learn and develop these skills by emulating the good example of teachers and mentors, and by practicing them in their work situations.

The starting point for such improvement is the manager's own performance in leading coworkers to achieve a vision. Every manager serves as a role model, teaching by example. If a manager is not communicating well with peers and with the person to whom he or she reports, if there is no one else who knows the manager's job, and if the manager doesn't have a sense of how he or she contributes to fulfilling the organization's objectives, then the manager needs to address his or her own beliefs and style of management first.

Respecting Privacy

Elder care is not a common topic at the office water cooler. There are a variety of reasons for this, including our fears about aging and the commonly felt confusion that surrounds elder care. Many working mothers and fathers will talk freely about child care issues with peers or supervisors. There seems to be a better comfort level in chatting about what Johnny's pediatrician is like or where to find trained baby sitters in town. Elder care is often a more private topic. Therefore, the manager needs to respect the confidentiality of information shared by workers.

When a worker shares his or her concerns with a supervisor, it is good practice for the supervisor to ask whether or not the information has been shared with others in the work place. If he or she has not shared a situation with others in the office, the supervisor should not do so either, taking care that confidential conversations not be overheard. Maintaining the level of confidentiality the worker desires is key to establishing and maintaining trust.

As with any job performance issue, electronic or hard-copy communications about or documentation of the issue should be stored in a secure manner. This means keeping personnel records in a separate, locked file and making use of security measures in the organization's computer system, changing access codes or passwords regularly to assure that only authorized personnel can obtain this information. The manager needs to know the organization's policies related to confidentiality of employee information and to adhere to those policies.

CONFLICT AND ELDER CARE

By taking proactive steps like building trusting relationships, providing educational information, and making it easy for working caregivers to obtain the support service information they need when they need it, many elder care related conflicts at work can be avoided altogether. However, even a talented manager working in an organization that does an effective job of providing these supports will need to deal with some elder care work conflicts.

Conflict, real and potential, is at the heart of work/family balance issues. The astute manager will realize that work/family conflicts will emerge, and consequently will develop strong conflict management skills. To do so, the manager needs to distinguish between positive and negative conflict.

Negative Conflict

Murphy describes situations in which negative conflict predominates in this way:* "Individuals view others as adversaries. They are more concerned about protecting themselves and less, or not at all, concerned about the basic human rights of others. They try to win at all costs and often see people as expenses rather than investments. They often take negative statements personally and do not try to elicit the true thoughts and feelings of others. They play mind games."[4]

Positive Conflict

In situations where positive conflict exists, "Individuals, with differing points of view and personalities, show mutual respect for each others' thoughts and feelings; they consequently develop effective partnerships. In short, they are supportive of one another. They are secure enough to communicate openly. They avoid playing mind games. Rather than taking negative statements personally, they assert themselves to achieve positive results."[5]

If patterns of negative conflict predominate, managers should look into training and education for themselves and their coworkers to change the cycle of conflict from negative to positive. The resources listed at the end of this chapter can provide a starting point for reversing the cycle. Conflicts need not be negative ones.

*Excerpts from Jim Murphy, *Managing Conflict at Work* (New York: Irwin/Mirror Press, 1994), p. 1. Copyright 1994 Richard D. Irwin, Inc. Reproduced with permission of The McGraw-Hill Companies.

The four-step process outlined in the next section provides a framework for managers and supervisors to handle those elder care related conflicts that cannot be prevented.

A FOUR-STEP PROCESS FOR EFFECTIVELY RE-SPONDING TO ELDER CARE CONFLICTS AT WORK

Murphy points out that "Conflict is a daily part of our lives. It can take many forms, from small encounters to full-scale battles. No matter what form a conflict takes, you can learn how to resolve and prevent it. The key to managing conflict is having the courage to take risks and to regularly practice techniques that will give you more control over your environment. . . . When you handle conflict, you not only put out fires, but prevent fires from flaring up."[6]

We have all fallen into the trap of "putting out fires," that is, simply reacting to one crisis after another. As many managers have learned over time, the process of continuing to put out fires without attempting to detect—or sniff out—potential problems before they become difficult to manage often results in personal burnout. Learning the skills and techniques for achieving a positive flow of conflict is essential for a manager's long-term effectiveness as well as higher self esteem. Being able to apply these skills in situations of elder care work/family conflict is particularly important because of the intensity and sometimes, volatility of elder care related conflicts.

These are the four steps for effectively responding to elder care conflicts:

1. Sensing conflict.
2. Establishing a common understanding of the problem.
3. Negotiating and innovating solutions.
4. Monitoring for needed changes.

There are at least five possible ways of dealing with conflicts at work: ignoring, repressing, demanding, negotiating, and innovating. The methods described in the following sections emphasize negotiating and innovating, but there are situations when ignoring, repressing, or demanding may at least temporarily make sense. These special circumstances are discussed under Step 3.

Step 1: Sensing Conflict

Bill, a manager at a large manufacturing plant, experienced an elder care related conflict last year as the deadline approached for completing his detailed annual departmental budget. Over the years, he and Anna, his administrative assistant, had worked together smoothly on the budget process. He anticipated upcoming changes and she compiled needed back-up information from a variety of sources. In the middle of the process this year, however, Anna did not seem quite as organized as usual. Also, she had called in sick with unusual frequency during the past winter.

Bill became angry with Anna when she submitted incomplete reports and missed target dates for steps in the budget process. He assumed that she had simply lost interest in her job and was avoiding responsibility. He kept his feelings to himself and did not try to sense or determine what was the true cause for Anna's change in behavior.

What Anna did not tell Bill was that her mother had been diagnosed with Alzheimer's disease and was becoming increasingly forgetful. Her mother could no longer safely live at home alone. Anna had organized a complex schedule of visits by friends, relatives, neighbors, and volunteer companions to cover the hours when her mother would otherwise be at home alone while Anna was at work. Creating and maintaining this scheduling system sapped a lot of Anna's energy. Despite her best efforts, sometimes the system broke down, and she had to stay home from work to fill in the time gaps.

Anna was not comfortable telling Bill about the situation. She felt nervous and guilty because she knew it was having an impact on her usual, highly organized approach to work. She noticed that communicating with Bill was becoming more formalized; there was not the easy back-and-forth banter that helped them both work together smoothly in the past.

One Friday afternoon, at the end of a particularly hectic week, Bill blew up. He verbally reprimanded Anna and demanded that she catch up on all her assigned research and submit an accurate report by next Tuesday. Anna burst into tears and quit her job on the spot.

Most people mistakenly believe that the first step in solving a problem is identifying the problem. Often, one cannot identify a problem until one first senses that a problem exists. In Bill's case, a valuable employee has left the organization and he has missed an opportunity to sense and resolve the underlying problem.

What potential conflict-starting clues should Bill have seen in the situation described above?

1. Bill incorrectly assumed that Anna had lost interest in her job and was, therefore, not as attentive as usual to the details of her budget support assignment. When he saw a recurring change in Anna's behavior, Bill might have spoken privately to Anna to understand her thoughts and feelings. Listening well might have helped Bill sense the presence of the underlying problem.

2. The change in communication pattern from easy-going to more formal might also have provided a clue to Bill that something was awry. Rather than acknowledging the change and talking about it with Anna, Bill withdrew further from the situation by becoming more rigid and formal in communications, setting the stage for a confrontation.

3. Bill might have become aware of his own unexpressed anger as an indicator that something was wrong. Even at the point of his "blow up" that Friday afternoon, Bill might have chosen to reign in his anger and not act on it. An alternative course of action would have been for him to sit down with Anna that afternoon, let her know of his feelings of anger and frustration, share with her the facts he had observed about her decline in work performance, and elicit Anna's thoughts

and feelings in order to better understand what factors were contributing to the change in her behavior.

Murphy cites five ways to improve sensing conflict on a daily basis:

1. *Be thorough*. Visualize how your actions or those of others will cause, or are causing, conflict. Ask yourself who, what, when, where, why, and how questions to determine potential, as well as present, sources of conflict.

2. *Give feedback*. The amount, accuracy, and timeliness of information that you can provide to an individual will help you understand that person's point of view. Sharing your thoughts and feelings *first*, in a nonthreatening way, often encourages others to tell you what is on their mind. Starting to talk about elder care concerns that you personally have or had could elicit information about your associates' problems with elder care.

3. *Get feedback*. Take the time to find out what your supervisor and associates are thinking and feeling. If a change in performance is noticeable to you, it is probably having an impact on others as well. Don't wait until the last moment to discover that trouble is upon you. Probe for more information by asking questions such as "How so?," "In what way?," "Why?," and "Can you tell me more?"

4. *Define expectations*. Meet on a weekly basis with your supervisor and/or associates to determine priorities for the upcoming week. Any major discrepancies between your expectations will alert you to potential conflict. It can be helpful for a manager and the work group to generate lists identifying what each expects. Differences between two parties' lists are potential grounds for conflict.

5. *Review performance regularly*. When supervisors and employees communicate openly about how they are (or are not) working together, they reduce serious conflict and build stronger working relationships. Every worker should participate in a review of his or her performance every three to six months. The review need not be in writing.[7]

Watch out for assumptions. There can be many reasons underlying a change in level of job performance. Elder care stress is just one possible cause. Don't jump to conclusions. A wise initial approach is to open up communication and learn more about what is really going on.

Step 2: Establishing a Common Understanding

Let us assume that the manager has sensed that an elder caregiving conflict exists. The manager has examined his or her own assumptions and obtained some feedback from the worker that elder care responsibilities are impacting his or her work performance.

The next step involves the manager and the working caregiver coming to a common understanding of the problem that exists. The manager needs to continue to make a distinction between the work place problem and the caregiving issues that are causing the problem at work.

From the perspective of the working caregiver, the work place problem (i.e., tardiness, lack of attention to detail, unexcused absences) and the caregiving issues may blend together as one. Caregiving situations may involve one or more of a variety of issues and challenges. For example, there may be conflicts among siblings regarding the amount and kind of care an ailing parent should receive, the parent may refuse to accept certain types of help, paid home care workers may not be showing up or they may not be performing their duties properly, or the cost of care may be exceeding the financial means of the parents and the working caregiver.

The Power of Denial

What the manager perceives as a job performance issue may be a manifestation of a breakdown in the caregiver's method of coping with a changing situation at home. Often, the caregiver may be in a state of denial regarding the situation outside of work: "When problems arise, family members often minimize a parent's unusual behavior, complaints, or increasing demands, as par for the course or part of normal aging. It is not unusual to deny anything is really wrong, even as circumstances change. At some point, however, wishful beliefs that things are normal cannot be maintained. Usually a critical event occurs that disrupts business-as-usual activities and coping patterns that have worked in the past. Whatever the critical event, it causes a number of feelings to surface, including fear, anger, anxiety, depression, and confusion. Concerned family members ask questions to obtain information and figure out what is wrong, but usually do not know where to turn for assistance.

For Cathy, the critical event was not her mother's first stroke. It was an interaction between her ten-year-old son, Dan, and her mother that occurred on Thanksgiving, several weeks before the stroke. Cathy and Dan were setting the table when her parents began an angry fight in the kitchen.

Cathy's mother barged into the dining room and screamed at Cathy that no one loved her and that she wanted to die. At that point Dan moved toward his grandmother and reached for her arm, saying "But I love you, and I won't let you die!" His grandmother slapped his face and shouted "I wish you were dead, too!" It was then that Cathy finally realized that something was drastically wrong with her mother, who had never laid a hand on anybody. She knew it was time to seek help.[8]

Fear, anger, anxiety, and confusion represent a powerful emotional mix. A caregiver experiencing such feelings may begin to find it difficult to maintain the usual routine in his or her life. The emotional impact of an incident like Cathy's, obviously, spills over into work.

In communicating with the caregiver, the manager may need to help clear a path through the emotional confusion. By focusing on the specifics of the job performance issues, the manager may help highlight the reality of a situation which the caregiver may not have recognized.

Focus on Performance

Sticking to specifics is essential. It is more helpful to say, "Sally, on April 4 you forgot to send off the articles you had collected for the editor of the employee newsletter. On the 11th, 12th, and 13th you arrived more than an hour late and you really looked beat. What's going on?," rather than, "You can't seem to remember things any more and you're late for work all the time." The former approach can help the worker take a careful look at what is actually going on and the reasons for the changes taking place. The latter approach may simply provoke an emotional, defensive response, based on the working caregiver's feeling of being threatened or attacked.

Job Performance Log

Catching people doing things right is a far more powerful motivator and morale booster than focusing on problems that need to be corrected. It is a good idea to keep a job performance log for each direct report. Managers can make regular notes in a notebook that is kept in a locked desk drawer or in a secure program on a computer. The log should include notes about the good things people have accomplished as well as recurring difficulties. Keeping a log allows the supervisor to quantify the positive and the negative aspects of performance and provide specific feedback. It is also a helpful reference for making deposits into one's Emotional Bank Account. In addition, it can be used to write a performance evaluation that represents a full year's performance rather than just the last few months, which is what many managers often remember to write about.

Ideally, a manager will develop a balanced approach, one in which he or she can express genuine concern for the individual situation while avoiding taking on the role of personal advisor. Although it is often upsetting and painful for the caregiver, calling attention to the reality of changes in work performance can sometimes serve as an important "wake-up" call, breaking through a pattern of denial. When this occurs, the floodgates may open, so be prepared for a possible outpouring of emotions.

What can a manager do if the employee does "lose it," emotionally breaking down in a meeting? At such a time, the most valuable action a manager can take is to validate the worker's feelings. If the manager has experienced similar emotional crises himself or herself, then the manager may feel comfortable letting the worker know that there is a shared understanding of the stresses such situations entail. At a minimum, the manager can maintain eye contact and nod affirmatively to signal empathy. Often, a meeting like this will conclude in one of two ways (1) The caregiver will calm down and regain perspective. In this situation, the manager can refocus the discussion to begin defining a common understanding of the problem. (2) The worker will feel embarrassed and uncomfortable about having shared an emotional outpouring. If this is the case, he or she is probably not ready to move on to defining the problem. In either case, the manager can suggest that both parties take a day or two to think about the situation and set a date to meet within the next work week to come to a mutual understanding of the problem. In addition, the manager should inform the working caregiver about the resources available to him or her within the organization and in the community. Drawing on the resources described in the appendixes to this book, the manager can write down the names and telephone numbers of two or more agencies or individuals that the worker can contact in order to obtain an objective assessment of the elder care situation in which he or she is involved.

Written Problem Statement

With the focus on job performance issues and not the specifics of the underlying elder care circumstances, the manager and the caregiver have a solid basis on which to mutually define the problem. It helps to write it down, although a verbal common understanding can also serve the purpose.

A useful problem statement should be as specific as possible. It should include the following:

- The name of the person or persons involved.
- The anticipated duration of the problem.
- The situation stated in terms that clarify work place requirements and the needs of the working caregiver.
- The person or group responsible for resolving the problem.
- The desired outcome or goal.
- A date by which the solution will be developed and implemented.

Here is a sample problem statement:

Mary Smith is a customer service representative. She reports to Ted Higgins, manager of customer service. Over the past six weeks, Mary has arrived late for work five times and has made several lengthy personal phone calls per week at work. These changes in Mary's normal work performance have come about because of her need to provide an increased amount of support for her ailing parents. Mary and Ted met to discuss the problem on February 27 and mutually concluded that for the next six months Mary needs time flexibility to fulfill this pressing family obligation. The customer service department needs to assure adequate telephone coverage during normal business hours, 8:00 A.M. to 6:00 P.M., Monday through Friday. By March 15, the customer service team, of which Ted and Mary are members, needs to develop a six month coverage plan that will meet both these needs.

A draft problem statement can be prepared by either the worker and/or the manager or supervisor. Both should take time to consider it carefully—usually, a day or two is sufficient. After making any needed changes so that the statement is mutually acceptable, both sign off on the statement. Then manager and worker can proceed with Step 3.

Step 3: Negotiating and Innovating

Having sensed that a problem exists and talked with the caregiver to define and agree upon a common statement of the problem, the manager is well on the way to helping the caregiver resolve the conflict. By following the first two steps, the manager, unlike Bill in the case example cited earlier in this chapter, has taken a proactive approach, neither ignoring nor repressing the conflict. By communicating directly with the working caregiver about how the job performance affects the situation, the manager has rejected the option of seeking a resolution through making demands. However, there are times when these methods of resolving conflict are appropriate.

Ignoring can be a responsible method to use when you find yourself in a situation where you are (1) too angry to talk, (2) gathering more information, or (3) developing a plan. Ignoring conflict in these cases, at least temporarily, is prudent.

When do people respond to conflict by repressing it? This occurs when one person doesn't want to hurt others' feelings. "The emphasis is placed on maintaining or strengthening relations with others even at the expense of the person who is doing the accommodating. There is a feeling that tranquility will win out if we just hide what bothers us."[9] In general, the only circumstances under which repressing is an acceptable response to conflict are those in which the conflict is unimportant, that is, it does not relate to your mission or values. In such situations, it may pay to let it go and move on to matters of substance. Since the stress related to elder care has to do with the ongoing quality of working relationships, it rarely falls into this category. The manager who finds himself or herself repressing or ignoring such conflicts might benefit by taking a look at his or her own feelings about aging in Chapter 2, as well as his or her own management style and assertiveness skills (see the Resources section at the end of this chapter).

Making demands is a last-resort form of conflict resolution. It makes sense only when a conflict cannot be resolved by other means or when time constraints demand an immediate decision. "This method, when often used, is an abuse of authority. (Demanding) people use their power to start and resolve negative conflict. Usually inflexible, they would rather tell people what to do than try to influence them. Demanders will do whatever it takes to win. Relationships are established only as a means to get whatever is needed. Loyalty is meaningless."[10] When is it appropriate to make demands? There are occasionally situations in which a working caregiver is totally unresponsive to a manager who has made reasonable attempts to clarify and state a problem. In such situations, the manager may legitimately demand that the two people meet with a third party, either the manager's boss or an employee relations professional in the organization in order to air the situation and to recognize the existence of a problem. Such a meeting may achieve the needed breakthrough in communication, paving the way for the manager and worker to establish a problem statement and a plan of action. In addition, it can result in a referral for counseling, a leave of absence, or other stress-relieving assistance for the working caregiver. In some instances, such a meeting will serve to bring an untenable situation to a head, resulting in transfer out of a given work unit or disciplinary action if the communication and performance impasse between manager and worker cannot be breached.

In many cases, work/family conflicts related to elder care need not result in the kind of communication breakdown described above. However, elder care issues and conflicts take so many different forms that it would be impossible to lay out a single approach for resolving such dilemmas. The manager, caregiver and the other members of a work team can craft solutions that work in a particular situation by using a combination of negotiation and innovation.

In using either negotiating or innovating techniques, the manager needs to remember basic caregiver needs, focus on the problem statement, and make use of outside resources, as needed.

Basic Caregiver Needs

As described in Chapter 2, caregiver needs fall into four basic categories: time, timely information, finances, and emotional support.

Time is a commodity that we cannot expand. The manager can, however, influence a caregiver to make better use of the time he or she does have. The organization may or may not have formal policies regarding flex time or job sharing. In cases where policy exists, the manager needs to know how much leeway is allowed in interpreting and applying the policy. In organizations that have no formal policy in this area, the manager needs to ask him or herself what will work in the context of achieving the work unit's mission and goals. A manager needs to trust his or her judgment in defining working arrangements, always focusing on the desired performance results.

Timely information refers to obtaining advice and help from the myriad sources available to the caregiver and his or her aged parent. Contrary to some people's beliefs, it is definitely a strength to ask for help. These include health care, social service, government, and community agencies. The manager is not in a position to be an expert on the resources available through this "aging network." However, by becoming familiar with the breadth and scope of help available (see Chapter 5), the manager can often assist the caregiver in knowing the right place to contact for information and help in assessing a situation. At a minimum, the manager should know where to access a list of key local agencies and sources of aging services information, as described in Chapter 6. The organization may decide that it wishes to take positive action to minimize the downtime and other productivity losses that accompany the caregiver's time-consuming task of finding and evaluating needed services by, for example, engaging an elder care consultation and referral (C&R) service to cut the red tape for caregivers. (These and other options are detailed in the section titled Organizational Response in Chapter 5.)

Financial support will often be an issue for caregivers. The manager's responsibility does not extend to developing strategies for arranging affordable elder care. Caregivers in a financial bind can turn to several sources for help. Aging service experts, legal and financial advisors can help a caregiver determine which present and future costs may be borne by public programs, what role private insurance should play, and how to tap the equity of an elder's home to help pay for care, as well as many other options. Caregivers should let the experts provide sound advice on financing needed elder care. Some organizations do incorporate long term care insurance and limited elder care reimbursement in their benefits plans. These are discussed along with other organizational responses in Chapter 5.

Emotional support is essential. Whether a caregiver is aware of it or not, the stresses and strains of coping with parent care can be emotionally draining. Is it appropriate for a manager to become the caregiver's primary source of emotional support? Probably not. However, a manager can make a positive contribution to the caregiver's efforts to cope with stress by regularly acknowledging the fact that he or she is experiencing a difficult situation.

Negotiation is a give-and-take approach to resolving conflict which requires people to focus on working as a partnership or team to beat a problem. The conflict is often resolved by parties starting at opposite ends and ending up somewhere in or near the middle. Through the use of principled negotiation, two or more individuals can develop solutions which decide issues on the merits rather than through a haggling process focused on what each side says it will and will not do.

Innovation is a process that taps people's creativity to solve problems. Mike Vance and Diane Deacon define creativity as "the making of the new and the rearranging of the old in new ways."[11] Innovating can deliver results when the people involved are skilled in achieving consensus, share a common understanding of the problem, allow enough time to complete the method, share a determination to practice innovation as part of their day-to-day work, and build in methods to elicit feedback from everyone involved in the conflict.

Principled Negotiation

There are four basic points to principled negotiation:[12]

1. Separate the people from the problem.
2. Focus on interests, not positions.
3. Generate a variety of possibilities before deciding what to do.
4. Insist that the result be based on some objective standard.

In the example of Bill and Anna described earlier in this chapter, Bill notices that Anna's performance of her tasks related to preparing the annual budget begin to slip. Bill could have chosen negotiating instead of repressing as a method of response. Instead of stewing over the problem, becoming more distant as he repressed his anger, and eventually blowing up—resulting in Anna quitting her job—Bill might have sensed something was wrong and engaged Anna in a dialogue about the specific incidents. Let us look at how the situation might have played out differently.

Separating the person from the problem. By focusing on and discussing the series of late arrivals, increased sick days, and late submission of reports,

Bill and Anna separate the performance problem (tardiness and a decrease in job performance) from the person (Anna, the worker and caregiver).

Focusing on interests, not positions. By developing a problem statement that they both agreed upon, Bill and Anna focus on their interests. Bill's interest is in submitting a budget in a timely and accurate manner while retaining a good coworker; Anna's interest is in arranging needed care for her mother while retaining her job. They develop a problem statement which reads, "Our problem is that, for the next two months, Anna will need the flexibility to arrive later than usual, leave earlier than usual, and occasionally work part-time rather than full-time, so that she can fulfill a family obligation. At the same time, our department needs to prepare and submit its annual budget and this requires concentrated administrative support. Bill and Anna will take responsibility for sorting out the routine, nonbudgetary tasks in Anna's job from those related to budget development, so that Anna can be relieved of the budgetary tasks for this budget cycle."

Generating a variety of possibilities before deciding what to do. Now is the time for innovating. Bill and Anna focus on the problem statement. They each develop a list of ideas for how the problem can be solved. Before their next meeting, they each write down their ideas. Here is their combined list:

1. Hire a temporary administrative assistant to take on the routine secretarial tasks so Anna can concentrate on budget preparation tasks only.
2. Hire a temporary administrative assistant to take on budget preparation tasks, so that Anna can concentrate on routine secretarial tasks only.
3. Arrange for someone from the accounting department to be temporarily assigned to assist Bill in gathering the needed budget information.
4. Request and obtain an extension of the normal deadline for budget submission.
5. Temporarily reduce Anna's working hours to part-time.
6. Train another administrative support person in Bill's department to understand and assist with the process of gathering the needed information from many sources.
7. Adjust Anna's work schedule to include four hours of "core time" per day, allowing for her to arrive or depart up to two hours earlier or later than usual, as needed.
8. Arrange for Anna to "job share" with someone else (from her own department or the accounting department), allowing her and someone else to reduce their hours, while still assuring that all her job tasks are accomplished.
9. Arrange for Anna to take a leave of absence to sort out her family situation before returning to full-time work.

Insisting that the result be based on some objective standard. Bill and Anna have both thought of ways of reconciling their interests. They both value their ongoing working relationship. How will they decide which alternative or alternatives from the list of possible solutions they have developed is fair and practical? An effective way to avoid a battle of the wills at this stage of problem resolution is for one party to insist on some objective standard or standards for the result. In most supervisor–worker relationships, the manager or supervisor holds most of the negotiating power; however, this is not always true. The relative negotiating power of two parties depends on how attractive to each is the option of not reaching agreement. Can Bill afford to have Anna quit? What are the costs to him and the company of recruiting a competent replacement, training the individual, and integrating the replacement into the team?

The most obvious place to look for a standard of fairness are the policies and practices employed elsewhere in the organization. Since their organization has no formal policy on work/family scheduling flexibility, Bill and Anna decide to refer to precedents, that is, actions that have been taken in similar situations.

In a discussion with the employee relations representative, they learn that other department heads have allowed for rearranging work schedules for administrative assistants as long as the department has been able to manage the total cost of the new arrangements within their approved administrative support budget for the year. Bill and Anna agree that this is a fair criteria for evaluating the options that they have identified. They also agree that it is reasonable to assure that any solution allow for preparation and submission of the budget on time, since this is a requirement of Bill's job.

Bill and Anna have thus identified and agreed upon two objective standards to apply to the potential solutions: (1) the cost of the new arrangement must fit within the department's annual administrative support budget, and (2) the new arrangement must not detract from completing budget preparation on schedule.

Using these two criteria, Bill and Anna eliminate options 1 and 2 since they conflict with the separating the person from the problem; there are no funds available in the administrative support budget for temporary staffing. They eliminate option 4 because Bill's boss has made it clear there will be no extensions to the budget preparation deadline.

Managers working in organizations with fifty or more employees need to provide information about leave of absence provisions under the federal Family and Medical Leave Act (FMLA) (see Chapter 5 for a summary of the provisions of this law). Bill and Anna consider a leave of absence but Anna feels she can find an accommodation by adjusting her working hours. They both acknowledge that there could come a time when a leave of absence would make sense.

Together, they decide to try a combination of options 3 (arrange for someone from the accounting department to be temporarily assigned to assist Bill in gathering the needed budget information), and 7 (adjust Anna's work schedule to include four hours of "core time" per day, allowing for her to arrive or depart up to two hours earlier or later than usual, as needed). Anna cannot afford to reduce her working hours at this time. No one on the staff in her department has the time or skills needed to pick up some of her responsibilities, but someone in the accounting department is willing to take on the budgeting preparation assistance and the accounting manager agrees to her taking this on temporarily.

Bill and Anna agree that the process they have used generated good ideas for possible future use as well. As a result, Bill sensed a solution for future problems and is going to build in cross-training his own staff in his objectives for next year. It also got Anna thinking about a possible job-sharing arrangement, if and when she can afford to switch to part-time.

Bill and Anna acknowledge that the situation with her mother is unpredictable. They agree to try out the new work arrangement for three months and evaluate how it is working at that time.

Step 4: Monitoring for Changes

Elder caregiving often involves uncertainty about the duration of a situation or an issue. It is important to build in check points at specific time intervals, as Bill and Anna have done in the example. These check-in points allow everyone involved to monitor whether the situation has changed and to measure the impact that the new arrangement is having on performance of the individuals involved and the organizational unit.

When it does come time to evaluate the situation, the manager needs to focus on performance issues: Are objectives being met? Have the work routines of others been affected? Are there unanticipated benefits or problems related to the new arrangement?

Team Approach

The previous case example focuses on a situation primarily involving two individuals, a supervisor and supervisee. If Bill and Anna worked as members of a team, the process would have involved the whole group from the beginning. Everyone on the team would help define the problem, participate in developing innovative alternative solutions, set criteria for evaluating the solution to be chosen, and monitor the pluses and minuses of the chosen solution at time intervals they all agreed upon.

Building work/family balance issues, like elder care, into job design, work processes, and organizational structures makes strategic sense. This approach means that coworkers who serve on the same team would determine elder care balance issues for themselves.

When Things Do Not Work Out

In the course of a working relationship, supervisor and supervisee (or members of a work team) jointly determine whether there is a good fit between the individual and the job that needs to be done. Dealing well with an issue as personal as elder caregiving needs to take place in this context.

If the manager has dealt with the working caregiver's situation in the manner described in the four-step process, then he or she has focused on job performance, not the personal issues of the working caregiver. When all reasonable accommodations have been made, it is the manager or supervisor's responsibility to determine whether the individual's performance meets the organization's requirements. Sometimes a transfer to other duties on a temporary or permanent basis is a viable option.

If it becomes necessary to dismiss the employee, the manager or supervisor should do so only on the basis of documented, consistent inability to meet job performance standards. In taking such action, a manager should be sure to follow the steps in the organization's policy on firings, such as written and verbal warnings and grievance rights.

The art of people management requires the manager to exercise good judgment and fairness. Most elder care related performance issues can be resolved through a combination of adjusting working hours, reassignment of duties, referral for help from community resources, or use of leave time with or without pay.

Managers who make the investment in improving the skills they need to effectively sense and resolve elder care work conflict issues will reap rewards far in excess of the time and energy they devote to the task.

NOTES

1. Stephen R. Covey, *The Seven Habits of Highly Effective People* (New York: Simon & Schuster, 1989), 188–190.

2. Covey, *Seven Habits*, 188.

3. Richard Hamermesh, "Good Management Isn't about Fads," *Boston Business Journal* 14 (January 1997): 10–11.

4. Jim Murphy, *Managing Conflict at Work* (New York: Business One Irwin/Mirror Press, 1994), 1.

5. Murphy, *Managing Conflict at Work*, 15–16.

6. Ibid.

7. Murphy, *Managing Conflict at Work*, 4–5.

8. Donna Cohen and Carl Eisdorfer, *Caring for Your Aging Parents* (New York: G. P. Putnam's Sons, 1995), 12–13.

9. Murphy, *Managing Conflict at Work*, 64.

10. Ibid.

11. Mike Vance and Diane Deacon, *Think Out of the Box* (Franklin Lakes, N.J.: Career Press, 1995), 67.

12. Roger Fisher and William Ury, *Getting to Yes* (New York: Penguin Books, 1981), 10.

Chapter 5

The Organizational Response

The future we predict today is not inevitable. We can influence it, if we know what we want it to be.

—Charles Handy

This chapter, in combination with the policy, program and service descriptions included in Chapter 6, provides the manager with a step-by-step method for building an organizational response to the needs of working caregivers. It begins by telling why it makes sense for an employer to make an investment in developing an elder care response. Next, key planning factors are listed. The presentation moves on to a review of a seven-step process for developing an initiative tailored to the manager's particular situation, and then concludes with a list of ten low cost or no cost supports that every employer can implement immediately.

WHY INVEST IN DEVELOPING AN ELDER CARE RESPONSE?

Researchers conservatively estimate that $11.4 billion per year is the figure that reflects the annual cost in lost productivity, increased turnover, and higher medical premiums related to elder care in the work place. Employers who have made a commitment to elder care as part of their work/life initiatives report that their investment in these supports pays for itself many times over by reducing the negative affects that can occur in relation to elder care. To date, there are no longitudinal studies which can conclusively prove that elder care supports improve working caregivers' productivity or reduce direct costs. However, several large employers have evaluated their efforts in conjunction with national elder care vendors. The following example illustrates one method being used by employers to quantify the impact.

Quantifying Results

Researchers at WFD, the nation's largest work/family consulting firm, report that employees across industries save approximately fifteen hours each time they use Lifeworks, WFD's comprehensive work/life balance program which includes an elder care consultation and referral component. The estimated average number of hours saved is based on surveys of over 30,000 employees who use WFD's consultation and referral service (C&R) serving child care and elder care needs. Survey respondents attribute these savings to three C&R benefits: (1) expert consultation, (2) reduced employee legwork for confirmed referrals, and (3) provision of information and tools to organize the process.

In calculating the value of these benefits, the WFD model assumes that 80 percent of the time saved by the employee would have been spent during work hours. Using this assumption, a large regional bank that uses WFD as its work/family vendor calculates the savings related to its expenditure on its work/life initiative using the following formula:

$$X = C \times h \times L \times p$$

where

X = total cost savings

C = number of C&R cases in a year

h = average number of hours saved per C&R case

L = average labor cost per hour

p = percentage of work time saved

Last year, 1,012 of the bank's employees used the service and the average hourly wage for their workers was $28.00. Thus, the annual savings attributable to the bank's Lifeworks programs was $332,551. To calculate the net savings, one would need to subtract the cost of the contract with the vendor for the consultation and referral service. In the case cited above, the company realized benefits valued at several times the cost of its annual contract fees.

Example: Calculation of Annual Savings

Step One

Number of C&R cases (or other unit of service)	1,012
Average number of hours saved	× 14.67
Total Hours Saved	**14,846**

Step Two

Cost per hour	$ 28
Total hours saved	× 14,846
Total Labor Savings	**$415,689**

Step Three

Total labor savings	$415,689
Assuming 80% of hours saved are work hours	× 0.80
Total Corporate Savings	**$332,551**

Realistic Expectations

Every organization presents a unique set of factors and circumstances which need to be taken into account in developing an effective elder care response. Chapter 2 pointed out that the foundation for sound program planning is an assessment of preparedness of the individual manager and of the organization. Assuming that the manager has undertaken this assessment, program planning can proceed.

Realistic expectations about the number of workers who will make use of elder care offerings are essential. The data from large employers that have offered elder care resource and referral (R&R) services for several years indicate that use of these services remains relatively modest. The major R&R vendors report use rates of 1 percent to 3 percent and occasionally as high as 5 percent per year. There are several reasons that may explain this low rate of use: (1) general discomfort on the part of workers with discussing issues related to elder care, perhaps rooted in the feeling that addressing such an issue is a private, family matter; (2) corporate cultures in which it is still not really acceptable for employees to admit the presence of such outside family demands on their work time and priorities; (3) ineffective communication techniques for reaching those workers who need the information and assistance most (e.g., the working caregiver in a crisis situation); and (4) the fact that the demographic "bulge" in the number of working caregivers is just beginning to make itself felt as baby boomers enter the sixth decade of life. Whatever the reasons for this phenomenon, it is important not to overestimate the number of users of an elder care initiative. Realistic expectations will lay the groundwork for a program that can grow and change over time.

PLANNING FACTORS

Plans must also take into consideration four other factors affecting organizational structure and performance.

- The size, location, and characteristics of the work force
- Equity in work/life benefit offerings
- Organization of the human resources function
- Elder care resources availability in the community

This chapter begins with a review of these factors, followed by a description of a seven-step process for organizing a response to elder care needs. The third part of the chapter presents examples of successful initiatives from a variety of organizations. The concluding segment highlights future directions for elder care development.

Size, Location, and Characteristics of the Work Force

The number of workers employed in an organization will often dictate the degree of formal structure required. For example, very small enterprises (fewer than fifty workers) may choose to handle elder care issues on a personalized, one-to-one basis, dealing with the particulars of each situation in light of the needs of the work unit and the specific needs of each individual. Because organizations of this size are exempt from the requirements of the Federal Medical and Family Leave Act (FMLA), there are fewer mandates, less reporting, and more opportunities for flexibility. Small employers generally offer fewer formal benefits and rely more heavily on informal channels of communication.

Mid-sized organizations (up to 2,000 employees) need to pay closer attention to equity issues since their work forces are likely to include groups of workers with divergent priorities and needs. These organizations rely more heavily on formal channels of communication, but can enjoy a degree of flexibility in work/life benefit planning that may not be possible in larger organizations. They can experiment more easily, perhaps adapting more quickly than their larger counterparts to the changing needs of their workers.

For large employers (2,000 or more workers), close attention to formal channels of communication and consistent implementation of corporate work/life initiatives become imperative in order to assure consistency and fairness of benefits administration, as well as to collect information for evaluation of results across the organization.

Organizations of any size may avail themselves of low-cost approaches like those described at the end of this chapter. In particular, all employers can benefit from pooling their resources and their concerns in local collaborative relationships with elder service providers either through specific, targeted task forces or through such membership groups as local chambers of commerce.

Location influences program planning in several ways. A company that operates at a single site may draw heavily on the elder care resources in that geographic area, emphasizing collaboration with local agencies and professionals. An enterprise with far-flung offices and facilities might find it more valuable to work through a "broker" organization that maintains accurate, up-to-date listings of elder services resources throughout the nation so that the right kinds of help can be found regardless of the location of the working caregiver or the care recipient.

Organizations that employ an older-than-average or predominantly female work force are more likely to experience elder care as a top priority issue. Such characteristics as education level and type of work performed also need to be taken into consideration in program planning. For example, a company at which the majority of workers perform blue collar jobs in a production facility is often not able to provide the same level of flextime or flexplace (i.e., telecommuting) for each individual worker that is possible in an office employing primarily professional and technical workers. However, there are other ways to allow for flextime options for working caregivers in such situations, as illustrated in the case example citing the practices of the Fel-Pro Corporation later in this chapter. Coberly suggests five basic screening questions a manager can use to conduct a quick assessment of the level of elder care responsibility among workers.[1]

1. Is a large proportion of the work force comprised of women?
2. Is the average age of employees forty or above?
3. Do middle-aged employees, particularly women, have an above-average incidence of arriving late, leaving early, or being absent?
4. Have middle-aged employees, particularly women, retired earlier than expected or planned?
5. If the company offers an Employee Assistance Program (EAP), have EAP staff received requests for assistance with problems related to caregiving?

Equity in Work/Life Benefit Offerings

The increase in the number of women in the work force has dramatically changed the patterns of daily life for American families, including the issues and concerns that workers bring to their place of work. The needs of those workers who are caregivers for elders are a subset of a wide spectrum of concerns, such as dealing with needs for infant and child care, coping with the crises of adolescent children, caring for an impaired child or younger adult, and managing household chores. Historically, work/life initiatives at most employers have started by addressing child care needs, then evolved to include areas such as elder care.

The program planner needs to consider the fact that "families" take many forms today. According to the U.S. Bureau of the Census, over 60 percent of workers do not have children and this percentage is steadily creeping upward. Consider the situation of Helen, a childless worker. She is one of two employees in her seven-worker office who does not have young children at home. It often falls to her and the other childless coworker in her group to stay late or come in on holidays when the parents in her office have to pick up the children from day care or rush home to care for an ill child. Yet the office's work—handling media relations for a major nonprofit organization—often demands odd hours and short deadlines. "It happens a lot," says Helen. "On the one hand, I feel for the parents' situation and I want them to take care of the needs of their families. But when you're stuck with the additional workload, it becomes a delicate emotional balancing act."[2]

To avoid resentment building up among childless workers, employers need to take an approach that assures equitable treatment for all. The likelihood is high that any given worker will, at some point, face the work/family balance issues related to elder care. Employers will want to tailor their benefits packages to include the flexibility needed to match each worker's needs at a specific time in life. Such life cycle benefit programs recognize the diversity of today's work force and the fact that workers' needs change over time.

Organization of the Human Resource Function

A company's approach to organizing its human resources function will impact program planning for elder care. Two key factors include the company's approach regarding direct administration versus outsourcing certain functions, and the degree of staff specialization within the organization.

A small but growing number of companies employ specialists in the area of work/family benefits administration. In the absence of such a staff specialist, the responsibility for defining elder care issues and priorities will often fall either to a single manager who may or may not work in the human resources area or to a task force comprised of representatives of several organizational units. Whoever takes the initiative, it is critical for the planning process to include all those who have a stake in the program's success. This includes top management, financial managers, and line managers, as well as human resources personnel. Once a program has been defined, the organization will need to decide whether its elder care initiative will involve an expansion of the responsibilities of existing company personnel, hiring new, specialized staff, outsourcing to an elder care vendor, or some combination of these three options.

Elder Care Resources Available in the Community

While long distance caregiving is a real and very stressful part of life for a segment of working caregivers, the majority of caregivers live within a twenty minute commute of the elders for whom they provide care, and only 6 percent of care recipients live more than two hours away from their caregiver.[3] This means that, especially for those employers whose workers are concentrated in one, or a few, distinct geographic areas, the variety, quality, and quantity of elder care services available in the communities where major facilities are located becomes an important program planning factor. Rural areas, for example, present special challenges in addressing elder care needs because there are fewer formal agencies and programs available. Outside of major metropolitan areas, community care of the elderly relies more heavily on volunteer services and the involvement of churches, and civic and fraternal organizations. In such situations, an adequate supply of needed elder care services can be an important factor. See the case studies presented in Chapter 6 for examples of the kinds of partnership initiatives that an employer can undertake with local providers to develop the elder care services needed to assure the success of an employer-based elder care program.

THE SEVEN-STEP PROCESS FOR IMPLEMENTING AN EFFECTIVE ELDER CARE RESPONSE

Regardless of the size of the organization, the following seven-step process provides a workable framework for planning and implementing an elder care response. The activities described in this program development process may be undertaken by the manager, by a consultant, or by a consulting team. Whichever approach is chosen, Step 1 needs to be performed by a manager within the organization.

Step 1: Justify Attention to Elder Care

The first task of the manager planning an elder care program is to demonstrate to top management that such an initiative is reasonable and in the organization's self-interest, and to gain support for devoting time, energy, and resources to tackling the issue. This entails educating oneself and others about the needs of working caregivers and formulating the case for taking action, based on the conditions affecting the organization. In the earliest stages, a good way to focus thinking is to confer informally with other managers and supervisors to find out whether elder care issues are surfacing for them, and if so, what kinds of needs and situations they are encountering. Collecting a few case examples and being able to describe them can help make the issue concrete and understandable.

Drawing on their preliminary research, managers should prepare a briefing paper that succinctly makes the case for action. Suggestions for preparation of an effective briefing paper include the following:

- Keep it short and to the point. If possible, use a single-page memo format.
- Apply the facts and figures presented earlier in this book to illustrate the strategic significance of the issue for the organization, adding information specific to the company's circumstances and business goals.

- Link the statement of case to specific, strategic issues that top management has already identified as important.
- Give some idea of the impact elder care can have on the company's financial performance.
- Include specific recommendations for short-term action.
- Attach a clear, detailed case example describing an experience of one of the company's employees, illustrating the impact elder care can have on individual performance and on the functioning of a team or department.

A sample briefing paper is shown on page 89. The manager can use the briefing paper as a reference document and as a focus for discussions with affected parties.

In a smaller organization, the manager can proceed informally. Using the briefing paper as a focus, a manager should talk with the company owner or chief executive and obtain the go-ahead to formulate a proposal for consideration. In a larger organization, attention should be focused on the issue by including it as a departmental goal. The earlier a manager can obtain support of top management, the better the chances of the initiative's success.

Stakeholders Meeting

Soon after obtaining top management's recognition of elder care as a legitimate concern, a manager needs to involve others in the process of program development. One way to get started is to convene a stakeholders' meeting, or a gathering of representatives of all the groups in the organization that will have anything to do with implementation of an elder care initiative. In addition to human resource and benefits administration personnel, this might include high level executives who would have an interest in the outcome of the initiative, people administering existing functions like an Employee Assistance Program, community relations staff, and the corporate medical director. The group should include all those persons whose support is essential to the successful start-up and operation of the elder care initiative.

A sample agenda for the first meeting of the stakeholders group might include the following:

1. A review of planning steps taken to date, including the support obtained from top management.
2. A presentation of information about the general trends that are driving consideration of elder care as an important work place issue (see Chapter 1).
3. The solicitation of input regarding special issues and concerns for program planning from the perspectives of the meeting participants.
4. A discussion of the proposed next steps (quantifying the need), including the description of the timetable for action and the cooperation and support needed from the participants.

Universal Electronic Components Corporation
15 Electron Way
Martinsville, TX 78750

To: Barry Martin, VP Human Resources
From: Karen Lockwood, Benefits Administration
Re: Issue Brief: The Business Impact of Elder Care
           April 30, 1998

Scope and Significance of the Issue

Recent conversations with line managers and supervisors reveal that a growing segment of UECC's 2,500 employees are experiencing the demands of caring for elderly relatives. Driven by the general aging of the population, this trend affects our cost of doing business through losses in productivity (national estimates are $1,500 to 3,000 per year per working caregiver), increased turnover, and increased health care costs. In addition, recruitment and retention is affected because businesses competing for the same pool of skilled workers in UECC's primary manufacturing location are incorporating elder care in their benefit offerings.

Relevant Current Policies and Practices

The comprehensive benefits review conducted three years ago identified child care issues as an important recruitment and retention concern, and several changes in policies and benefits practices were made to better accommodate employees' needs in this area, most notably UECC's support for the development of a child care center adjacent to the main manufacturing plant. With the exception of the dependent care spending account option that can be used to set aside pretax income for care of an elderly dependent, UECC has not formulated a specific response to the needs of employees related to elder care.

Recommendations

I recommend that we include a departmental objective for FY 1999 relating to elder care, authorizing research which will tell us (1) how many employees are now facing, or will in the next five years face, elder care responsibilities, (2) the specific types of assistance that employees feel would help them better balance such responsibilities with their work responsibilities, and (3) the strengths and weaknesses of current UECC policies and benefits offerings as they relate to elder care needs of employees. I look forward to discussing this with you, including my ideas for ways to conduct the needed research at minimal cost to UECC. I can provide data from national studies regarding cost impact.

Attachment: Case example of a fifty-six year old electrical engineer employed for the past seven years in the R&D department who is caring for his eighty-six year old mother in his home.

Step 2: Assess the Need

The program plan needs to include an estimate of how many workers in a given organization will have elder caregiving needs and what kinds of needs they have. There are at least three ways to develop this estimate. Depending on the size of the organization and the resources available to conduct research, the manager may wish to make use of all three techniques:

1. Draw on the research results from other organizations and apply percentages.
2. Conduct a formal survey of the organization's workers.
3. Collect information informally within the organization.

Drawing on Other Companies' Experience

Are there guidelines that can be drawn from other companies' experience? A few large scale studies have been conducted to estimate the prevalence of elder care as a work place issue. In each of these studies, the researchers looked at the number of workers providing general elder care and those providing intensive, hands-on elder care.

As pointed out in Chapter 3, the distinctions among the different levels of caregiving intensity are important for program planning. General elder care may include such forms of assistance as emotional support via personal visits or telephone calls, helping with managing finances, shopping and house cleaning help, providing financial support, researching and arranging for services, providing transportation, and escorting an elder to doctors' appointments. Research has shown general elder care represents over two-thirds of all elder care provided by family caregivers (working and nonworking).[4] Intensive, hands-on elder care includes helping the elder with such activities of daily living as bathing, dressing, and eating.

Collecting Information Informally

Much valuable information can be collected by talking informally with key personnel and a sampling of workers in the organization. In smaller organizations, this may provide enough information to structure the organization's response. The manager should make a list of basic questions that need to be answered in order to move forward with the planning process. Here are some examples:

- How often has elder care surfaced as a reason for distractions at work or for an unusually high number of absences from work?
- What are the specific kinds of elder care work/family balance situations that have come to your attention?
- If the organization were to offer one or two kinds of help for working caregivers, what would they be?

Sources of response to such questions might include the following:

- One-on-one interviews with a sampling of managers and supervisors.

- Self-selected focus groups of workers who are family caregivers.
- Employee relations staff.
- Employee Assistance Program staff.

In addition, the manager should make use of the organization's informal communications grapevine. As Deal and Kennedy remind us, "Everyone . . . has a job—but he also has another job. This 'other job' won't get stamped on a business card, but that doesn't matter. In many ways this work is far more important than budgets, memos, policies, and five year plans. . . . This network is actually the primary means of communication within the organization; it ties together all parts of the company without respect to positions or titles. The network is important because it not only transmits information but also interprets the significance of the information for employees."[5] These storytellers, priests, whisperers, and especially secretarial sources can all provide valuable information for elder care planning. Specifically, the manager should ask around to find out which employees have been active in volunteer activities like a United Way appeal or the local Alzheimers Association Memory Walk fund raiser. Other staff will often turn to such individuals to share their caregiving experiences or to seek information on sources of community services for their own needs or those of fellow employees. Working caregivers may also confide in these individuals regarding particularly positive or negative experiences they may have had with their supervisors in their attempts to balance their work and caregiving responsibilities.

To Survey or Not to Survey

Some organizations are reluctant to conduct a survey of employees on an issue like elder care. Timing may be an issue; one survey following immediately on another may diminish the likelihood of a good return. Also, some employers feel that asking workers about elder care may raise expectations for action on the issue.

The positive benefits of conducting a survey outweigh the potential negatives. Survey results provide the organization with a firm grasp of the facts for program planning and a baseline for evaluating the future performance of any elder care initiative. In addition, survey results can be used as an educational tool, increasing the sensitivity of management personnel to the issue.

Because elder care issues are often personally sensitive, confidentiality of survey responses must be maintained. The program planner can increase the respondents' confidence in this regard by engaging an outside organization or consultant to conduct the survey and tabulate results. A statement regarding the confidential nature of responses should be included on the survey tool itself.

A survey need not be lengthy to produce useful results. The sample survey instrument in Appendix B includes thirty-five questions and takes about fifteen minutes to complete. All employees should be encouraged to respond whether they currently have elder care responsibilities.

The entire survey process, from the announcement of the survey through preparation of a written report summarizing the findings, will take about ten weeks. The following list of tasks and related time frames are presented as a guide for survey implementation.

Task	Time Frame
1. Announce the survey purpose and the date on which it will be distributed to employees, using employee newsletter, memo to managers, e-mail postings, etc.	1 month in advance
2. Print a sufficient quantity of the survey tool and a cover letter, emphasizing respondent confidentiality.	2 weeks in advance
3. Distribute survey tool via mail and e-mail or intranet posting.	specified date
4. Issue reminder memo, e-mail notices, urging employees to return completed questionnaires.	1 week after
5. Deadline for submission of completed questionnaires.	2 weeks after
6. Complete tabulation and analysis of results.	1 month after
7. Issue report to management detailing findings.	6 weeks after
8. Report findings in newsletter, on intranet.	2 months after

The cost of conducting a survey can vary widely, depending on whether the organization uses an outside firm or undertakes the research internally. Managers should check with an organization like the Society for Human Resources Management for inexpensive survey research software products available. However, as mentioned earlier, workers may not be as forthcoming and candid in their responses to an internally generated and tabulated survey. Sources of research help include benefits planning and consulting firms and academic research centers. Small, local firms specializing in work/family balance or elder care concerns may be able to conduct a survey at lower cost than larger, national groups simply because they operate with lower overhead. A college research center on aging may be a cost-effective alternative. In any case, when considering use of any outside research help, one should inquire as to the organization's or individual's research qualifications and track record.

• What are the credentials of the person who will oversee the research?
• What experience does the researcher have in work/family issues, and specifically, in elder care?
• Ask for references, other employers, or other organizations who have made use of the organization's research work.

Using Survey Results for Program Planning

A survey can provide valuable information about such general topics as the extent to which workers regard the organization as "family-friendly" and workers' awareness of current company offerings related to elder care support. In addition, the information obtained from a survey using a questionnaire like the sample in Appendix A will help the program planner focus an elder care initiative by quantifying

- the number or workers who currently, or in recent years, have had elder care responsibilities.
- the number of workers who anticipate taking on elder care responsibilities in the near future.
- the kinds of help they are providing to elders, and the difficulties, if any, they are experiencing in providing needed assistance.
- the amount of time they are spending in providing elder care.
- the extent to which elder care is affecting work attendance and performance.
- the number of caregivers by level of intensity of caregiving.
- the extent to which long distance caregiving is an issue.
- the kinds of help working caregivers feel would be most helpful in addressing their situations.

Survey results need to be summarized in an easy-to-read format, discussed with the stakeholder group, and included in reports to top management.

Step 3: Review Existing Policies, Programs, and Practices

Next, a manager should review the organization's existing personnel policies, programs, and practices from the point of view of the working caregiver. There are three good reasons to do this. First, such a review can help target areas where relatively minor changes can make a substantial difference—for example, providing for short-notice access to flextime (i.e., the ability to vary the specific hours of work within a given week or month to accommodate caregiving demands at home). Second, the review may identify ways to improve communication of policies and programs that are already available to working caregivers. Summarizing relevant offerings in a booklet, newsletter articles, or via postings on electronic bulletin boards, can make existing resources better known to caregivers. Third, a review can help set priorities for incremental improvements. For example, if the organization has no provisions for flextime or leave benefits, the manager may wish to focus first on improving these important sources of caregiver support before moving on to developing other facets of an elder care program.

Twenty-One Areas for Review

There are at least twenty-one areas to be included in the review, including policies, practices, benefits, and services. The listings below use definitions developed by Neal et al., the Ontario Women's Directorate, and Kamerman and Kingston:[6]

Policies and Practices. These describe the formal and informal ways in which employees' work and leave schedules are handled. Policies provide the parameters for dealing with certain situations. Generally, except for paid leave (e.g., sick, vacation, or personal), policies involve no direct compensation or cash benefit. Practices are the concrete actions taken by decision makers, usually managers or supervisors, in relation to the organization's policies. The actual practices of managers may or may not conform to the organization's policies.

Benefits. These are forms of compensation, direct or indirect, that provide (1) protection against loss of earnings; (2) payment of medical expenses associated with illness, injury, or other health care needs; or (3) paid release time for vacations or personal needs. Benefits may also include provision of payment (full or partial) for other services, such as legal, educational, or dependent care services.

Services. These are specific programs provided directly by or through the employer that address a particular employee need in a specific way. Services are a tangible form of help but not direct compensation. Neal et al. suggest the following framework. Services differ from benefits in that the employer, rather than the employee, chooses the approach (i.e., specific service) to meet a given type of need; thus, when the employee chooses the type of service to be purchased, subsidized, or discounted to meet his or her particular family-related needs, the support itself is considered a benefit. When the employer makes this choice, the support is considered a service. Using this framework, the following list designates subsidies and discounts for care as both benefits and services.

In their pioneering work on balancing work and caregiving, Neal et al. produced a comprehensive listing of potential supports that an employer could put into place to help caregivers find the balance they seek. The following list of supports can be used to review an employer's existing policies, benefits, and services in relation to elder care program development:

Part-time job options
- part-time work
- job-sharing
- voluntary reduced time
- phased retirement

Flextime

Flexplace (telecommuting)

Relocation policies

Sick, vacation, or personal leave

Parental or family leave

Medical or emergency leave

Health, dental, life, other insurance

Unemployment insurance, workers' compensation

Federal or state tax credits (publicizing of)

Dependent-care reimbursement plan

Subsidized dependent-care reimbursement plan

Long-term care insurance, other insurance

Subsidized care or vouchers

Discounts for care

Education

Resource and referral

Counseling

Case or care management

On-site care center

Resource development

In conducting the review the manager should use the following checklist to gather essential information about each of the following items:

1. Does the organization now offer this type of support?

   If yes

   a. What is the specific definition of the support as it now exists?

   b. Does the current definition of this support match the specific needs of working caregivers as defined in the needs assessment?

   c. How might the definition or scope of the support be changed to more closely match identified needs?

   If no

   d. Would addition of this support potentially meet a high priority need of working caregivers as identified in the needs assessment?

2. For each of the supports currently provided,

   a. how is the support communicated?

   b. to what extent is the support utilized by working caregivers?

Upon completion of the review, the results should be tabulated and displayed in an easy-to-read chart format, with an accompanying narrative detailing each of the current offerings. The report should rank the supports in priority order, giving the highest priority to those which most closely match the needs identified in the assessment.

Step 4: Assess Options for Program Development

The completed assessment of working caregivers' needs and the review of existing personnel policies and benefits serve as the foundation for the next step in program development. At this point, the manager needs to produce a list of recommended options for action.

The chart summarizing existing offerings listed earlier serves as a starting point for listing options. The manager now needs to critically appraise the contents of this list in light of trends in the business environment. This is the time to conduct a benchmarking survey.

What are competitors offering? What are the best practices in the industry across the nation? The program and benefit definitions and case examples in this book can serve as an information base to which the manager can add current data from the marketplace. If the manager is working with a consulting firm in developing the program, the managing consultant should be able to provide such information. If the manager is proceeding without the aid of a consultant, there are several quick, inexpensive ways to obtain this information:

- Review research conducted by the trade association(s) representing your industry regarding current trends in compensation and benefits. Do not limit research to review of the published results, however. Make a telephone call or two to the appropriate staff at the association. Such industry insiders can often shed additional light on trends and refer you to companies that offer best-practice models.

- Conduct a search on the topic via the Internet. There are dozens of web sites containing information on a wide variety of personnel management and benefits administration topics. For example, each of the major benefits consulting firms maintains a site on which they publish summaries of their own and others' research.

- Review the content of relevant professional journals for the past two years. In some cases, the manager can accomplish this on line, as well. Any major public or university library also carries these periodicals.

- Call colleagues in similar positions at other companies. Sometimes these conversations can uncover information about innovative approaches that have not yet gained wider recognition through publication or dissemination on the Internet.

Maintain a file on industry trends and practices. Storing all the information obtained in a single location will make it easier to conduct a thorough review later.

Once satisfied that the benchmarking effort has identified all the options that deserve consideration, the manager should evaluate the potential impact that each of the options might have. The evaluation might include such factors as match with identified needs of the organization's working caregivers; the number of workers likely to be affected; the cost to the organization; and the degree of complexity involved in developing and administering the offering.

By looking at each option from several vantage points, the manager will begin to identify those which make sense in a given situation. Some managers will be comfortable making a "seat of the pants" judgment regarding which options should be ranked higher than others. Other managers may wish to use an analytical approach that quantifies the relative value of each option (e.g., assigning a numerical value to each option related to whether the option is likely to have "high," "low," or "medium" impact in each area). Using such a system, a total score can be tabulated for each option, thus producing a rank ordering of priorities for action.

Regardless of the method used, the manager will want to separate the list of options into three groups:

1. Higher priority: options which deserve more attention at this time
2. Lower priority: options which may warrant future attention
3. Removed from consideration

After grouping the items into these categories, the manager should add those in the higher priority category to the chart listing existing policies, benefits, and services developed in Step 3. Next, review every item on the combined list, developing as much detailed information as possible regarding each item, including

- the estimated number of employees who would be affected.
- projected costs.
- how the new items will link with existing policies, benefits, and services.
- implications for equity across the entire employee population.
- estimated time frame for implementation of revisions or additions.
- special considerations (e.g., needed linkages to community organizations, or special communications barriers to be overcome).

In developing this information, the manager will need to make assumptions about cost and utilization. For example, the list might include an emergency back-up care service for which the manager has no actual operating information. If so, include whatever information can be obtained from the experience of another company operating a similar service. Extrapolate that company's utilization to the work force at hand, with some upward or downward adjustment if there is a significant difference in key characteristics of the employee group (e.g., one organization has a much higher proportion of middle aged women than the other). Avoid getting bogged down in an overly time-consuming pursuit of detailed data. Focus on gathering relevant information that is readily available. Maintain a running list of the assumptions used and the additional data that need to be collected. The objective is to present a coherent overview of the major components of the elder care initiative.

The result of work accomplished in Steps 3 and 4 will be a detailed report, organized as follows:

- findings of the results of the needs assessment.
- analysis of current policies, benefits, and services in light of the needs of working caregivers, with recommended changes.
- a list of new options recommended for implementation, with estimated cost and impact for each.

Step 5: Recommend an Action Plan for Approval

Once the report in Step 4 is complete, the manager needs to take a step back from the work and gain perspective on the work accomplished so far, and take the time to solicit feedback from others. Four specific ways to gain valuable feedback include the following:

1. Send copies of the report to members of the stakeholders group (or other small group of representative managers and workers) and solicit comments in writing or via telephone or e-mail, by a specified date.

2. Convene a meeting of the stakeholders group, and send a copy of the report to each member in advance of the meeting. At the meeting, start by asking whether anyone feels that an important option has been completely omitted from the list. Then, proceed to review each option on the list, soliciting reactions and suggestions as to the accuracy and appropriateness of the rank order and content of the recommendations.

3. Conduct a few informal discussions with working caregivers and describe the top priority initiatives being considered. Solicit input as to whether the recommended actions would be truly helpful or not. If the reaction is positive, stimulate suggestions for specific ways in which the actions might be refined in order to implement them effectively. If the reaction is negative, try to find out the specific, practical reasons that the caregivers consider the initiatives ineffective. Avoid scrapping any one initiative completely until you have explored the ways in which it might be modified to improve its effectiveness.

4. Consider sharing the document with a colleague in a noncompeting company or industry. A useful technique is to ask that the reviewer "put on the hat" of your company CEO. Most reviewers within the company will offer comments from their individual perspectives, whether they be managers, budgeters, or human resource management experts. Somewhere along the review process, someone needs to think like a CEO, providing the manager with an assessment of the initiative from a high-level, strategic perspective. A trusted fellow professional may identify shortcomings and pitfalls that you cannot see from within your organization. Alternatively, a colleague may simply confirm that you have developed the finest possible proposal for your situation.

The objective in seeking feedback is to gain as many perspectives as possible. Go back to your original document and reconsider each item in light of the comments offered. Even if the review does not result in changing a single word of the report, the manager will have strengthened his or her stance in presenting the recommendation by having anticipated many of the questions and concerns of the CEO or other final decision maker.

Next, prepare the final version of the report. A sample table of contents should look like the following one:

1. Executive Summary
2. Acknowledgments

3. Results of Needs Assessment Survey: Working Caregivers

4. Analysis of Current Policies, Benefits, and Services

5. Recommendations for New Supports for Working Caregivers

6. Benefits Realization Analysis

7. Action Plan

Attachments: Needs Assessment Survey Tool; Data Sources and Assumptions Used for Projections

Items 3, 4, and 5 of the table of contents correspond to the segments developed and refined in Steps 3, 4, and 5 previously mentioned.

The executive summary lays out the rationale and the key facts in a format that gives the CEO or other decision maker enough information to assess whether or not it will be prudent to authorize its implementation. Write this section so that it stands on its own, that is, if the decision maker does not have time to look at any other information in the report, he or she will have obtained the gist of the proposal. In a page or two, highlight the key elements of the plan: (1) its strategic significance for the organization; (2) the specific needs of working caregivers identified through research; (3) the key recommended changes in policies, benefits, and services; (4) the costs and benefits involved (benefits realization); and (5) the time frame for implementation.

It is very important to give recognition to persons inside and outside the organization who contributed to the recommendations in an acknowledgments section. If the manager is authorized to implement the plan, their cooperation will be needed. If the plan does not go forward, those who contributed to its formulation will have received some recognition for the time and energy they contributed to the work. The manager who remembers to thank others for their help is more likely to receive a positive response the next time help is needed.

The section on benefits realization analysis tells what benefits the organization will gain from the elder care initiative, the time frame over which it will realize those benefits, and their dollar value. The analysis should include subsections that project the costs of the recommended changes and additions over a multiyear period and state the hard and soft benefits to be derived. Examples of hard benefits include projected decreases in quantifiable costs such as turnover and health benefits expenditures and increases in productivity. Soft benefits include improved morale and positive public and community relations.

The action plan presents a list of quantifiable goals and related action steps with specified completion dates for each. Each goal and action step should specify the person responsible for its accomplishment, as well as the resources required. The actions should encompass all those activities essential to the successful implementation of the initiative, covering a time span of six months to one year, depending on the requirements of the particular plan. The degree of specificity of the action steps will vary with the size of the organization and the agreement between the program planner and the person(s) who has authorized preparation of the report. In larger organizations, the action plan may simply consist of a list of key goals with implementation steps to be determined after general approval of the initiative. In smaller companies, the CEO may wish to see the full set of specifics included with the set of recommendations. The sample goal statement and related action steps shown below would be appropriate within a medium-sized company (i.e., one with 2,000 or more employees working within a multidepartmental structure).

The following is an action plan that includes all elements.

Goal:	To offer telecommuting as a work option.
Responsible:	Director of Benefits Administration (DBA)
Completion Date:	April 1 (6 months after adoption of overall plan)
Resources:	Time of DBA, Benefits Analyst (BA), and manager(s) of department(s) for pilot site(s); printing costs for communications materials.

Action Steps

1. September 1: DBA issues memorandum to all department managers
   - Defining the proposed options for telecommuting and its link to productivity issues for working caregivers.
   - Inviting one or more departments to participate in a pilot program to test the model.

2. September 15: DBA conducts informational meeting for interested department managers regarding telecommuting option.

3. September 15: BA develops data collection tools for analyzing impact of pilot program on department operations and drafts program description materials for participating employees.

4. October 1: Deadline for responses from interested department managers. DBA selects one or more sites to pilot test the telecommuting model.

5. October 15: DBA conducts meeting with selected department managers at which BA describes methods for data collection and evaluation of the telecommuting pilot project, solicits suggestions for changes to draft communication pieces for employees.

6. November 1: Announcement of telecommuting option for employees in pilot groups. Data collection begins for three-month pilot period.

7. February 15: BA compiles and DBA issues report of findings from three-month pilot project, soliciting input of participating employees and department managers.

8. March 1: DBA issues report with recommendations regarding implementation of telecommuting as a companywide option.

9. March 15: VP of Human Resources acts on recommendations above, setting parameters for policies governing companywide implementation.

10. April 1: DBA oversees rollout of companywide telecommuting option.

Presenting the Plan

The manager should expect to make an in-person presentation of the recommendations for addressing elder care issues. If possible, the written document described above should be presented to the decision maker in advance of a presentation, so there is an opportunity to formulate questions for discussion or perhaps to solicit additional information which the program planner can bring to the presentation session.

Use the following checklist to prepare for the in-person presentation and follow-up. Depending on the size of the organization, the actual presentation may be formal or informal. Even in a very informal situation such as a one-to-one meeting between the manager and the business owner or CEO, the manager should prepare an agenda for the meeting and guide the discussion so as to cover each point. The checklist assumes that the manager will be making a formal presentation to a group of two or more executive decision makers.

1. Confirm availability of appropriate room. Be sure it is of adequate size for the number of participants and includes availability of needed audio–visual equipment (i.e., screens, projectors) on date and time of presentation.

2. Confirm that each invited participant has received the formal notice of the meeting and the action plan report at least one week in advance of the presentation.

3. Determine the specific decisions that need to be made at the meeting in order to move the project forward. Build these into the agenda.

4. Prepare an agenda for the meeting. Plan for a one-hour meeting. Specify time frames for each item on the agenda. Limit the formal presentation to no more than twenty minutes, allowing for most of the available time to be used for discussion.

5. Prepare visuals summarizing key points and recommendations. These may include (a) short video clips which provide policy context for the recommendations (see Appendix C for sources); (b) case examples of employees within the company (signed releases should be obtained from any workers for whom personal information is included); and (c) graphs, charts, or slides illustrating key points.

6. Prepare handouts for distribution. The handouts should be kept succinct and include the same information that will be highlighted in the visual presentation. Prepare extra copies of the full report to have on hand for those participants who may not have brought their copies and wish to reference specific details.

7. Rehearse the presentation. Find a quiet place, at home or at work, and conduct a full "dress rehearsal," including set-up and operation of the audio–visual (AV) equipment. Time the presentation and pare it back, if necessary, so that it does not exceed twenty minutes, including any video clips. Be prepared for AV failure. Be sure the handouts contain all points contained in the AV. For case examples presented via video, prepare a written description of the facts and circumstances of one case example that you can read in the event that the video cannot be shown.

8. Arrange for a record of the meeting to be kept. Either plan to keep your own notes or arrange for secretarial staff or another meeting participant (if appropriate) to keep minutes of the session.

9. On the day of the presentation,
   - Arrive at the designated room one hour in advance.
   - Adjust the physical setting as needed. Know how (or obtain assistance from someone who does) to dim and raise lighting, adjust heat or air conditioning and arrange seating to facilitate viewing of visuals.
   - Set-up and test operation of AV equipment at least thirty minutes before the start of the meeting. This will allow an opportunity to obtain AV personnel assistance, if needed, in advance of the start of the meeting.
   - Confirm availability of an adequate supply of handouts.
   - Personally greet each of the participants upon arrival.
   - Start and end on time.
   - Acknowledge the assistance of those individuals who have been particularly helpful in developing the plan.
   - Keep track of the time.
   - Keep the group focused on the agenda.
   - During the last fifteen minutes, courteously but firmly inform the group of the time constraint. Summarize the decisions that you understand to have been made (if any). If decisions have not been made, politely remind the group of the need to act on key recommendations. If it is apparent that there is insufficient time to make needed decisions, suggest two alternative dates and times for a follow-up meeting.
   - At the close of the meeting, thank attendees for their participation and confirm understanding of the follow up actions, dates for completion, and who is responsible if agreed upon action vary from those included in the plan.

Follow-up the presentation with a report to relevant parties, including those who may not have attended the meeting. The report should summarize decisions made at the meeting, particularly noting any modifications to the recommendations in the plan, and specify the agreed-upon follow-up actions, persons responsible, and dates of completion, if they vary from the action steps in the plan.

Step 6: Implement the Plan

The manager who has followed and successfully accomplished the activities in Steps 1 through 5 will be in a strong position to assure smooth implementation of an elder care/work balance initiative. Successful implementation of the plan requires effective delegation of the necessary level of authority and responsibility; assignment of adequate resources; cooperation of affected managers and workers; and effective communication of the content and purpose of the plan, including training of managers and supervisors.

Effective Delegation

The first and most important step is to assure that the person responsible has the necessary level of authority to carry out the implementation. Assuming that the adopted plan includes detailed action steps, this should not be a problem. If the activities require hiring new staff, job description(s) should be prepared, drawing on the goals in the plan. If existing staff will handle implementation, then the specific responsibilities should be built into job descriptions and/or included in team or departmental objectives, as appropriate.

Adequate Resources

If the manager has followed the format recommended above, the action plan adopted by top management will have included authorization for the specific resources required to implement the plan. Nonetheless, it is a good idea to prepare a memorandum, addressed to those controlling access to the required resources, to assure the availability of those resources within the agreed-upon time frame. This includes staff time as well as budgetary resources (e.g., funding for services purchased under contract from a vendor of elder care services).

Cooperation of Others

The importance of involving affected parties early in the planning process is critical to obtaining their cooperation and support for implementation. Having listened to others and incorporated their views and suggestions, the manager who has employed the recommended planning process will have removed many potential barriers to proceeding with implementation in a spirit of cooperation.

Effective Communication

To be effective, communications efforts must include training and education of management personnel, as well as the repeated delivery of consistent messages about the purpose and content of the elder care initiative.

Whether the elder care approach selected is a simple, basic one, like providing information to working caregivers and allowing a little more flexibility in arranging working hours, or more in-depth, like offering consultation and referral services and financial reimbursement for elder care, the organization needs to invest in training its managers to improve their handling of elder care issues.

Importance of Management Training

The program's success will hinge on the active support and cooperation of management personnel who supervise or lead teams of workers. Without their support, the program's utility for working caregivers will be limited. As Wagner et al. point out: "Conducting training of supervisors and managers regarding caregiving burden and the stress associated with caregiving makes the supervisor more sensitive to the issues confronting her or his employees who are caring for an older person. Training should be on going and not occur only when an elder care program is initiated. This training should be designed to enlist the cooperation of supervisors as referral sources for employees. . . . Training supervisors minimizes the likelihood that they will undermine the elder care initiative by discouraging the caregiver's participation . . . (e.g., asking the employee to finish a task rather than attend a caregiver seminar during lunch). Training also increases the likelihood that they will be supportive of employees who are caring for an older relative. Supervisors can also play an important role in reinforcing information about services in the community . . . by reminding employees of services or discussing with the employee possible options for help in providing care."[7]

Communication Techniques and Messages

Every worker, regardless of level of responsibility, needs to understand the ways in which he or she can make use of the organization's policies, practices, and benefits to better balance work and family life. Methods for disseminating such information to workers in the organization might include the following:

- Highlighting elder care at new employee orientation sessions and in employee handbooks.
- Including a notice or article, fact, service listing, or case example relating to elder care in every issue of the employee newsletter.
- Posting reminders on electronic bulletin boards and incorporating elder care information on intranet web pages devoted to benefits issues.
- Taking advantage of such events as Older Americans Month (May) or National Caregivers Week (the week after Thanksgiving) to highlight caregiver issues by holding informational fairs in collaboration with local elder services agencies, offering seminars, or the like.

Communications need to focus on three basic messages:

1. *Caregiving is a normal part of life.* It is important to recognize that workers take on the role of caregiver. As pointed out in Chapter 3, most elder caregivers do not identify themselves as caregivers. Recognition of the reality and legitimacy of this dimension of a person's life is a basic need. Without this recognition, the needs and concerns of caregivers remain invisible and unaddressed.

2. *Caregivers do not have to go it alone. Help is readily available.* Work place publications and notices need to inform working caregivers of the resources offered by the company and the community to assist them and those for whom they care. Presenting case examples of workers who have been helped can be effective in changing behavior and opening up new possibilities. Case examples and news and advice pieces should always include telephone numbers to call, intranet (or Internet) web sites to visit, books and periodicals to read, and where to obtain them.

3. *In this company, it is OK to strike a balance between caregiving and work.* Case examples are a particularly effective way to reinforce this message. Such stories need to highlight the experiences of workers from a variety of levels of responsibility within the organization. If executives are not comfortable taking advantage of elder care offerings to balance their own work/family situations and letting others know

about it, middle managers are unlikely to do so. Changing corporate culture involves sharing stories that demonstrate the organization's values in action.

Repetition of Messages Is Essential

Effective communication of the elder care initiative, not just when it is launched, but on an ongoing basis, is vitally important to success. Most people do not think much about the need to arrange elder care until a "crisis" occurs; then they often feel emotionally upset and overwhelmed by a situation they have not anticipated. Providing continuous information about elder care serves at least four important purposes. First, it lets workers know that the organization takes the issue seriously and wants workers to deal with elder care issues in a healthy way. Second, it encourages planning ahead—increased awareness will stimulate some workers to take a look at their family situations and make plans before their elder care situations reach a crisis point. Third, it puts valuable information in the hands of those working caregivers who are experiencing a crisis—they now know where to turn for help. Fourth, it reinforces the organization's values, helping to create an atmosphere in which it is OK to make use of benefits, policies, and practices intended to help caregivers balance their work and family lives.

A manager should draw on the results of the needs assessment and the comments and suggestions of everyone involved in planning to target communications to different groups.

Step 7: Manage for Maximum Effectiveness

An effective elder care program operates with clear goals and clear accountability for results. Like any other aspect of organizational management, everyone involved with the elder care program needs to be linked together in a continuous quality improvement process. This requires clear definition of processes from the start of the program, setting forth measurable and achievable results, monitoring program performance, and modifying the program as experience is gained. The overall goals are to assure that the "customers" of the elder care effort—the working caregivers and their coworkers—will find the program increasingly more useful, and the organization will realize the hard and soft benefits which the initiative is intended to achieve.

Managing for effectiveness starts with setting clear goals. For example, one goal might be to reduce the number of unanticipated absences, in order to minimize the disruption in work flow. To meet this goal, an employer might contract with a home care agency. For a retainer fee, the agency would assure that, on one hour's notice, it will dispatch a qualified home care aide to stay with an older relative who unexpectedly could not be left alone for the day. The cost of the aide's time might be split between the worker and employer. This would provide the worker some peace of mind, alleviate some of the cost for the emergency care, and avoid a day of absence from work.

The program manager must assure that a method of collecting data to measure progress is put into place. Someone must be assigned the responsibility to collect and report the data at predetermined intervals.

Program performance can be measured in terms of processes or outcomes. Process measures reveal such facts as how a service is delivered, how many units of service are delivered, and the number of persons making use of a benefit or service.

Tracking the number of workers who call an employer-sponsored elder care "hotline" to have their caregiving questions answered is an example of a process measure. Process measures cannot describe the impact a program has had on organizational performance or on the individual performance of service users themselves.

Outcome measures describe the impact a program has had on the sponsoring organization and on the program participants. Organizational performance outcomes are often more difficult to measure than outcomes based on personal experience.

The most common method of measuring outcomes for individuals is to measure their satisfaction level. A simple questionnaire can be sent to each user at a predetermined interval after use of the service. For example, each user of an elder care consultation and referral service might receive a questionnaire in the mail within one week of their initial use of the service, and then another questionnaire three months later to determine what longer-term impact, if any, the service has had on his or her caregiving situation and ability to balance work and family responsibilities.

To measure organizational impact of an elder care program, the manager must first identify some benchmark or standard against which to measure productivity, worker loyalty, or commitment to the company's success. For example, an organization might target reduction in the average number of days of unexcused absences per worker per year. The manager could then compare the average number of absentee days during the year preceding implementation of an elder care program to the comparable statistic at the conclusion of the first year of operation of the program. The problem with this approach is that is it is difficult to separate out the impact of one variable (for example, introduction of the elder care program) from the impact of many other variables that also impact the performance measure (in this case, the average number of days of unexcused absences from work). In any given year, a host of different variables might affect this statistic, including such factors as other kinds of work/family dilemmas (e.g., child care), an unusual clustering of personal issues unrelated to elder care, or an increase in drug and alcohol abuse problems.

Are there any rules of thumb that a manager can use to estimate the potential productivity benefits of a work place elder care initiative? As discussed in the beginning section of this chapter, the answer is a qualified "yes." Large employers who have offered elder care for a number of years report that their investment in this area has paid for itself many times over.

The following example from an accounting–consulting firm illustrates the potential cost effectiveness of elder care information assistance. A senior account executive was closing a multiyear contract negotiation worth over one million dollars. The day before her final presentation to the decision makers at the customer firm, her bedridden mother's live-in companion walked off the job without prior notice and, as the only adult child living near her mother, she was faced with staying home with her for a few days and jeopardizing the deal. Instead, she was able to call her employer's elder care consultation and referral "800" number. The counselor there researched services in her mother's town and arranged for her to interview three potential new companions after work that evening. She and her mother met the three candidates and selected one of them who had cared for another member of the mother's church. The daughter did not miss a day of work. The service cost the company less than $150.00.

First Tennessee Bank has reaped significant returns on its work/family initiatives. In 1993, the bank launched several programs to help its employees juggle the competing demands of their work and family lives. With four years of operating experience, the organization reported a surge in productivity and savings of over $3 million in turnover costs alone.

Baxter Healthcare examined its work/life initiative and found that the benefit components of its approach, especially work flexibility and specific programs like its elder care resource and referral service, have a high return on investment. "Employees who perceived the components as a benefit reported greater efforts to satisfy customers, increased focus on quality, greater commitment to business goals, recruiting friends and family to the company, and personally making efforts to enhance the company's image in the community."[8]

As illustrated, well-focused elder care support can deliver a quantifiable payback to the employer.

TEN LOW-COST–NO-COST ELDER CARE SUPPORTS THAT EVERY EMPLOYER CAN IMPLEMENT NOW

The good news for managers who work in small organizations and at companies with very limited budgets for employee benefits is that it is possible to implement many valuable supports for working caregivers at little or no cost to the employer. The list below highlights ten such supports. See the descriptions in Chapter 6 for specific information about each option and advice on implementation.

1. Resource Library

For an investment of under $500, an employer can make available a wealth of valuable information for working caregivers. (See Appendix C, Resources for Caregivers, for a listing of recommended books and tapes.) There are few things more valuable than providing the right book to the right person at the right time. This is especially true when it comes to coping with the complexities and stresses of elder caregiving. Once the library has been established, it is essential to publicize its availability on an ongoing basis. A simple way to accomplish this is to include a short description of one of the books or tapes in each edition of the employee newsletter under a heading like "Caregivers' Corner."

2. Eldercare Locator Service

Any resident of the United States can call a national toll-free number (800) 677–1116, and obtain help with identifying community resources for older adults anywhere in the country. Whether the older person in need of care lives nearby or in another state, the Eldercare Locator, funded by the federal Administration on Aging, can refer the caller to the information and assistance source in the elder's community. Employers should include this number in all human resources publications and include it in every newsletter article and related employee publications.

3. Flexible Work Schedule

Though this may require a measure of design creativity, it is possible to devise flexible work schedules even in companies with production employees or location and time-specific work needs. Two examples are: (1) IBM's flextime policy gives employees a two-hour window during the day for breaks, making it possible for working caregivers to make a quick trip home to check on an elder or run an errand; and (2) Fel-Pro, Inc. allows its manufacturing teams to set their own starting and quitting times, within certain parameters. See the Fel-Pro corporate profile in Chapter 6 for details.

4. Caregiver Fair

For the cost of a few dozen stamps, letterhead stationery, and a few dedicated hours of staff time, an employer can supply its working caregivers with a wealth of practical information about elder care resources available in the community. See the information presented in Chapter 6 for a step-by-step guide to organizing a fair.

5. Elder Care Seminar

There are dozens of agencies and organizations in nearly every community which employ talented, knowledgeable experts in various facets of elder care. These groups are usually more than happy to supply a speaker for a nominal fee, or free of charge, in order to gain exposure for the programs and services of the organization. Medicare, Medicaid, and Social Security are good topics for initial seminars. Contact your local Area Agency on Aging or State Unit on Aging (see Appendix A) to obtain names of good speakers.

6. Volunteer Recognition

Thousands of people devote volunteer time to such projects as friendly visiting, home delivered meals, and nursing home outreach. Tap the informal company "grapevine" to learn about the good works in which employees are engaged. Recognizing employees for community service activities costs the employer virtually nothing and provides an opportunity to simultaneously increase the visibility of community care resources among employees and enhance the employer's positive community image. Present an annual Elder Care Community Service Award, and publicize it internally and with the local news media.

7. Caregiver Support Group

Contact the local Area Agency on Aging, Senior Center, chapter of the Alzheimers Disease and Related Disorders Association or similar organizations and publicize the events taking place in your area.

8. Family Caregiver Awareness Week

Pick one week per year to congratulate family caregivers on their continued good work in supporting frail or disabled relatives. National Family Caregivers Week is usually the third week of November. Prepare a Family Caregiver Recognition Week banner and hang it above an information table in the employee cafeteria. For each of the five lunch hour sessions that week, invite one representative from each of five different elder service organizations to provide handouts and answer questions at the information table. The National Family Caregivers Association (See Appendix C, Resources for Caregivers) will provide brochures and copies of their newsletter, "Take Care." Call NFCA at (301) 942–6430.

9. Recognition for Managers

Corporate cultures change one story at a time. Catch people doing something right about supporting working caregivers and then tell others about it. Present case examples in the employee newsletter that illustrate how a manager or supervisor has accommodated a working caregiver's need to balance the work and elder care without sacrificing accomplishment of the organization's goals.

10. Managers' Information Session

Another way to make creative use of community resources is to invite a panel of local professionals to present an annual briefing for managers on a topic related to aging or elder care. Examples of topics might include legal issues (a local elder law attorney and a state representative explain recent legislative changes affecting working caregivers); health insurance (an HMO industry representative and a consumer advocate explain the choices available in Medicare managed care options); or mental health (a geriatrician from the local hospital and a protective services worker from the Family Service Society explain the difference between late life depression and dementia).

The final chapter of this book provides the manager with additional information to aid program development and implementation. Chapter 6 contains descriptions of elder care related policies, benefits, and services now offered by employers, along with corporate profiles and descriptions of model programs. The appendices supply answers as to where managers and working caregivers can obtain additional information and materials to support implementation of a successful elder care initiative.

NOTES

1. Sally Coberly and Gail G. Hunt, *The MetLife Study of Employer Costs for Working Caregivers* (Washington, D.C.: Washington Business Group on Health, 1995), 46.

2. Patrick Lee, "Juggling Act—No Kidding: When It Comes to Benefits, the Childless Often Feel Cheated," *Los Angeles Times*, 12 August 1996, 5.

3. National Alliance for Caregiving (NAC) and American Association of Retired Persons (AARP), *Family Caregiving in the U.S.: Findings from a National Survey* (Washington, D.C.: NAC and AARP, 1997), 8–11.

4. Ibid., 4.

5. Terence E. Deal and Allan A. Kennedy, *Corporate Cultures: The Rites and Rituals of Corporate Life* (Reading, Mass.: Addison-Wesley, 1982), 85.

6. Margaret B. Neal, Nancy J. Chapman, Berit Ingersoll-Dayton, and Arthur C. Emlen, *Balancing Work and Caregiving for Children, Adults, and Elders* (Newbury Park, Calif.: Sage Publications, 1993), 192–193; Ontario Women's Directorate (OWD), *Work and Family: The Crucial Balance* (Toronto: Consultative Services Branch, OWD, 1990); S. B. Kamerman and P. W. Kingston, "Employer Responses to the Family Responses of Employees," in *Families That Work: Children in a Changing World* (Washington, D.C.: National Academy Press, 1982), 144–208.

7. Donna L. Wagner, Michael A. Creedon, Joan M. Sasala, and Margaret B. Neal, *Employees and Eldercare: Designing Effective Responses for the Workplace* (Bridgeport, Conn.: University of Bridgeport, 1989), 42.

8. Alice Campbell and Marci Koblenz, *The Work and Life Pyramid of Needs: A New Paradigm for Understanding the Nature of Work and Life Conflicts* (Deerfield, Ill.: Baxter Healthcare and MK Consultants, 1997), 12.

Chapter 6

Options for Action

My advice is: Don't sit in your office and dream things up. Go out and
find out who's already doing good work in your community. A good place
to start is the local Area Agency on Aging.
— Tom Pugh, Baltimore Office, Social Security Administration,
and developer of a model caregiver information program

The growing field of work/life balance management is a dynamic and changing one. New approaches and combinations of management policies, practices, and benefits are emerging as organizations adapt to the requirements of
a global market place and the changing social contract for work.

The information in this chapter represents a snapshot, a picture taken at
one point in time, that illustrates the range of work place options that a manager should consider in developing an organizational response to the needs of
working caregivers. This snapshot begins with a description of activities now
being undertaken by employers in the United States. This segment is organized under the headings of Policies, Benefits, and Services and expands
upon the listing in Chapter 5.

The next section presents profiles of three different-sized employers, ex-
plaining how work/life offerings have evolved in response to changes in business conditions and in tune with organizational values. Model program
descriptions provide details regarding relatively new options, such as emer-

gency back-up care and caregiver support groups. The chapter concludes with an assessment of the developments that will likely shape elder care and work arrangements in the future.

CORPORATE POLICIES

Work Scheduling

Scheduling policy options include flextime, compressed work weeks, flexplace (telecommuting), regular part-time employment, job sharing, phased and partial retirement, V-time programs, and work-sharing.

According to a 1995 study of 1,050 major employers by Hewitt Associates, 67 percent of major employers now offer some form of flextime, up from 54 percent in 1990. The employers surveyed reported the following prevalence for different types of flexible schedule arrangements:

Flextime	73 percent
Part-time employment	65 percent
Compressed work schedules	21 percent
Work at home	19 percent
Summer hours	15 percent

In their guide to flexible work options, Olmsted and Smith include the following categories and definitions.[1] Each listing that follows* also includes one common concern (among several cited by the authors) expressed by managers considering introducing each option. A response follows each concern.

Flextime refers to work schedules that permit employees to choose their starting and quitting times within limits set by management. Once an organization has determined its official hours of operation, it needs to consider policies on the following:

- *bandwidth*—the time during which employees *may* be on site,
- *core time*—when employees *must* be at work,
- *flexible period*—the period of time within which employees and managers may negotiate starting and quitting times.

The options for flextime arrangements could include the following:

- starting and quitting times that are fixed periodically.

- starting and quitting times that can vary daily.
- variations in the length of the work day, with mandatory core time.
- variations in the length of the work day, with no mandatory core time.

Concern: Those working flexible schedules will not adhere to agreed-upon core work time commitments.

Response: Flextime is a privilege, not a right. If employees abuse the system, they can be required to return to the standard schedule.

Compressed work week is a standard work week compressed into fewer than five days. Common models include the following:

- the 4/10 compressed work week: four 10-hour days each week.
- the 3/12 compressed work week: three 12-hour days each week.
- the 9/80 compressed work week: four 9-hour days and one 8-hour day off.

This usually covers a two-week cycle and requires consideration of federal and state wage and hour laws for nonexempt employees.

Concern: If a manager's work unit requires five-day-a-week coverage, how can the manager authorize a four-day work week?

Response: Compressed work week schedules are most often used in conjunction with other scheduling arrangements. In some organizations, workers have developed a rotating coverage system.

Flexplace (telecommuting) is the practice of enabling regular employees to work at home or at an alternate work site during part of their scheduled hours (sometimes referred to as telework). Some kinds of work, especially creative and analytical work, can be done more effectively outside the office environment, with its ringing phones and other distractions and interruptions. Many firms which offer flexplace as an option make use of a process that requires the employee to submit a proposal in order to be approved for a telecommuting arrangement. A common proposal format might ask the employee to provide answers to the following types of questions:

- What business needs will be served by granting your request?
- How will customer service be affected?
- What is your proposed work plan and schedule?
- What kind of work space will you be using at home?
- What kind of work environment will you have at home (i.e., how will the employee dedicate the agreed-upon time for work if there are children or adult dependents there)?
- What kind of communication strategies will you employ?
- What in your work record would support your ability to work independently at home?
- Knowing this organization's philosophy and culture, what in it should encourage your supervisor to approve your request?

Concern: With an employee working off-site several days per week, the manager will have greater difficulty in evaluating the employee's performance.

Response: The emergence of new work options and arrangements has led to the development of a new supervisory style, one that encourages employees to take on more responsibility and that requires managers to provide more support than oversight. This new style of management focuses on achievement on mutually agreed-upon measurable objectives, rather than "line of sight" supervision.

Regular part-time employees are employees who regularly work fewer than the organization's established full-time hours. Their salary and benefits are prorated. Their time can be scheduled in ways that smooth the peaks and valleys of work flow.

Concern: Part-time employees may not be as committed to their jobs as full-timers.

Response: Because they feel their employer has responded to their needs, part-time workers are *more* committed than full-time workers. One large scale study found that a higher proportion of senior management rated productivity better for part-time than for full-time employees.[2]

Job sharing is a form of regular, part-time work that offers managers a creative solution for employees who request a change to part-time status. This option is particularly useful in providing part-time opportunities in higher-level positions, for example, in professional and managerial jobs with responsibilities that cannot be significantly reduced or split in two. Job sharers voluntarily share the responsibilities of a full-time position. Job sharing is different from regular part-time employment in that job sharing requires a team approach to performing responsibilities, often involves the job sharers in supervising one another's work, and can provide opportunities for cross-training and skills expansion in situations where the job sharing partners have different skills and experience.

Concern: Participants in job sharing arrangements may require more supervisory attention.

Response: When asked, most job sharers and their supervisors say there is *less* need for close supervision after the job sharers complete initial training and define methods of coordinating work.

Phased and partial retirement offers a way for senior employees to retire gradually by reducing their full-time employment commitment over a period of three to five years. Reduction in hours worked can vary from 10 percent to 50 percent. Some people cut back a few hours a day. Others cut back on days of the week. Still others take longer vacations. All are able to ease the shock from full-time work to full-time retirement.

Partial retirement offers senior employees the option to work part-time on a regular basis without establishing a future retirement date. In some programs, these workers receive partial retirement benefits to supplement wages. In others, they can return to full-time work if they wish to do so.

Concern: Older workers are inflexible when compared to younger workers.

Response: There is little or no research data to substantiate this view. In the absence of such data, managers should avoid basing decisions on stereotypes. The best approach is to try such options and monitor the actual results.

V-time program (Voluntarily reduced work time) is a time–income tradeoff program that allows full-time employees to reduce their work hours for a specified period of time with a corresponding reduction in compensation. Although this option can be offered on an ad hoc basis, it is more effective when offered as a formal program. V-time differs from regular part-time employment in that there is usually a time limit on the arrangement, and a process is defined for return to full-time status. Typical V-time program components include the following:

- Employees choose from several options of reduction in work time and pay, ranging from 2.5 percent to 50 percent.
- The agreed-upon schedule remains in place for a designated period, usually six to twelve months.
- An assurance is provided that the arrangement can be renegotiated or terminated at the end of the time period.
- The supervisor must authorize the employee's participation in the program.
- Time off can be taken either on a regular basis, as a reduced day or week, or in a block of time, such as extra leave or days off from work.

Concern: Employees on V-time may not be as committed to the organization as full-time employees.

Response: As cited in relation to regular part-time options, employees exercising this option are actually *more* committed to the organization because they appreciate the employer's responsiveness to their needs.

Leave time is an authorized period of time away from work without loss of employment rights. The absence may be paid or unpaid and is usually extended or taken for such reasons as family responsibilities, health care, education, or personal growth or career breaks.

Compliance with the Federal Family and Medical Leave Act

The federal Family and Medical Leave Act (FMLA) of 1993 has had a dramatic impact on employee relations, particularly in regard to issues related to responsibility for care of a family member who is seriously ill. FMLA applies to organizations with fifty or more employees. Workers who are eligible for FMLA leave may take up to twelve weeks of unpaid leave in a twelve-month period (as calculated by the employer). The aggregate twelve-week entitlement does not have to be used at one time and may apply to different conditions that meet the definition of a "serious health condition" for the employee or a family member. Leave to care for a family member must be permitted if it is "necessary" or "helpful" for the employee to be with the sick family member.

In 1995, the Wage and Hour Division of the U.S. Department of Labor issued the final regulations concerning implementation of FMLA. The regulations are lengthy and include significant changes in notice requirements and certification requirements for FMLA leave, the definition of a serious health condition for eligibility for leave, and the employers' job restoration duties upon completion of the leave.

The process of elder care program planning should include consultation with competent legal counsel on this issue. The U.S. Department of Labor offers a free FMLA guidebook for employers and provides answers to frequently asked questions about FMLA at its web site.

Flexible Leave versus Categorical Leaves

Also known as earned leave, flexible leave erases the distinction between the traditional categories of paid and unpaid leave, such as vacation, personal, and sick leave. Workers are given the flexibility to manage the use of their paid and unpaid leave time. Employers who have adopted a flexible leave approach usually require workers to plan in advance for use of leave, whenever possible. Flexible leave policies may also include provisions for job guarantees that go beyond the provisions required under FMLA. Here is an example.

During the last fourteen months of her mother's bout with terminal cancer, Betty, a human resources specialist, and her sister shared hands-on caregiving responsibility for her mother. Betty's employer, a health care organization, had adopted an earned leave policy several years earlier. The company's culture included a strong commitment to allowing workers to balance work and family demands. Betty says, "My managers were very flexible when I needed to take time off. For years prior to the enactment of FMLA, our organization had offered a very flexible system in terms of employees being able to take time off to take care of family members. With our earned time program, we don't really care why people take time off. It's there for whatever your personal needs may involve; you don't have to be sick. Our philosophy has been that earned time leave is theirs (employees') because they needed it. We figure that they are the best judge of how they need to use their time. In my own situation, my mother's illness was really dreadful, and there was a tremendous amount of time when I was out of work . . . and worrying about her a lot. We were able to off-load a lot of my work, with support from others in our department. And there were some deadlines that were simply forgiven. They were very flexible and very supportive of me. I was just never worried about putting my job at risk. Now, I'm back and working productively again. I think I would have had to consider resigning my position if my employer had been less flexible in accommodating my needs."

Time Banking

This arrangement allows a worker whose family or health situation requires an extended leave to draw upon the voluntarily contributed accrued paid leave of one or more other workers. A time banking system relies entirely on the voluntary participation and initiative of the workers in an organization. Administration of the system will include setting eligibility criteria and parameters for how much leave can be drawn by any given worker in a year. As a voluntary initiative, time banking requires involvement of a worker committee to assure ongoing communication and oversee the program in cooperation with the human resources staff.

Community Service or Personal Growth Leaves

These forms of leave provide employees with an opportunity to enhance personal learning while benefiting a community service agency and its clientele. Such leave may be paid or unpaid and may or may not be reviewed by a committee that conducts a selective application procedure. These types of leave recognize the value to both the employee and the organization of community service and time off to pursue personal interests. Community service leave can often be administered in cooperation with such local agencies as the United Way. Many nonprofit organizations serving elders can benefit from the expertise of a loaned executive.

Management Training Programs

In response to increasing diversity in the work place, many employers now offer training and education programs designed to increase workers' and managers' awareness of differences among employees and appreciate the value these differences add to the organization. Esty et al. list ten dimensions of diversity that need to be addressed, including two which relate directly to working caregivers—age and family situation.[3]

The continued aging of the population and the work force requires employers to include knowledge of aging and the family situations of working caregivers into such training programs. Such training and education may include an annual update to all managers regarding the ways in which company policies, benefits, and services can be of assistance to working caregivers; a segment on myths and realities of aging in personnel management training; and publications and occasional seminars to familiarize general managers with the range of community services and programs available to assist working caregivers and their relatives.

Resources for qualified trainers on these topics include academic centers on gerontology and aging, local area agencies on aging, work/life and elder care consultants and consulting firms, and geriatric care managers. See Appendix C for a listing of resources in this regard.

Corporate Giving Programs

Focused corporate philanthropy can enhance an employer's work/life balance efforts. In regard to elder care, corporate giving can play a role in improving the supply and quality of services. Locally, seed grants and capital grants can often assist established nonprofit providers to start programs that can be financially self-sustaining over time. On a national level, the American Business Collaboration for Quality Dependent Care offers an example of how a group of businesses can pool resources to improve systems of care for elders, as well as children and dependent adults. See Chapter 6 for an example of a successful consortium approach.

BENEFITS

Health Insurance

As noted in Chapter 1, caregiver stress can contribute to higher health care costs because when stressful conditions remain unrecognized and unaddressed, workers are more prone to experience accidents, injuries, and other health problems that require acute medical care interventions. Managed care plans that emphasize preventive care offer employers an opportunity to build in methods of identifying working caregiver stress earlier, thus avoiding some medical costs. The employer can encourage the managed care plan to target the needs of working caregivers by highlighting their caregiver concerns in health education newsletters to their members, offering support groups for working caregivers, and recognizing caregiver disorder as a legitimate reason for seeking mental health counseling as a covered benefit.

Since many managed care plans are expanding their product offerings to serve the Medicare population, employers can work with such plans to develop programs that capitalize on synergistic opportunities. For example, if an HMO is developing the capacity of its provider network to better address the needs of its Medicare members, the employer may be able to tap the HMO's increased geriatric expertise by informing working caregivers of the HMO's geriatric assessment services. Such assessments may be included as a covered benefit under the elder's Medicare HMO plan. The family caregiver derives the benefit of a better factual base for developing a care plan with the elder, at no direct cost to the employer.

Federal and State Tax Credits

The employer can use newsletters, handbooks, and intranet site postings to publicize the availability of federal and state tax credits available to working caregivers. Several states allow for tax credits or tax deductions for a portion of the cost of providing care for a dependent relative. State initiatives are generally linked to the federal dependent care tax credit, which reduces the amount of income taxes (but not FICA) the employee owes by a percentage of the expenses the employee has incurred as a result of his or her dependent care responsibilities. The percentage varies depending on the combined income of the employee and his or her spouse. The types of individuals for whom care may be provided and the types of expenditures eligible for favorable tax treatment are the same as those that apply to the Dependent Care Assistance Plan (DCAP), as specified in Section 21(b) of the Internal Revenue Code.[4] Though the DCAP and the dependent care tax credit can be used simultaneously, the same expenditures cannot be claimed twice. Furthermore, the amount of the tax credit is reduced by the amount excluded from income under a DCAP. The federal tax credit serves employees with dependent children to a much larger extent than it serves those with dependent adults or elders. Approximately 80 percent of the benefits claimed through this credit are for child care rather than for adult or elder care.[5] According to Neal et al., "The limited use of the tax credit for adult and elder care is due in large part to the restrictive regulations that govern its use. Allowable expenditures for adult or elder care include only those that 'assure the well-being or protection of the employee's qualifying spouse or dependent.' Care may be provided inside or outside the employee's home, although the dependent adult must regularly spend at least eight hours of every day in the employee's household. Moreover, all expenditures must be work related, and if the taxpayer is married, his or her spouse must also have been employed or have been a full-time student or a disabled qualifying individual. A further limit on use of the tax credit is that this care often qualifies as a medical deduction as well, and expenses may not be counted twice (i.e., as dependent care expenses and as medical care expenses)."[6]

Dependent Care Assistance Plan

A dependent care reimbursement account (formally known as Dependent Care Assistance Plan, or DCAP) is a type of flexible spending account. Canan and Mitchell define a flexible spending account as an account into which employees can allocate either their own pretax dollars or credits or flexible benefits dollars given to them by their employer to pay for certain expenses not covered under the employer's standard benefits package, such as medical, dental, legal, or dependent care.[7] Flexible spending accounts may be offered as an element of an employer's cafeteria plan. Alternatively, they may be made available by employers independently of the benefits plan as a service to employees.

Authorized under Section 129 of the Internal Revenue Code, DCAPs are a mechanism through which employers can help employees who have dependent care responsibilities and who must purchase dependent care or related services in order to be gainfully employed. DCAPs may or may not involve direct employer contributions. DCAPs are established for reimbursement of dependent care expenses incurred by the employee for household services or for the care of a "qualified individual" so that the employee can work. Qualifying individuals include children under the age of thirteen, as well as spouses or dependents who are unable to care for themselves, regardless of age, and who regularly spend at least eight hours each day in the employee's household. The U.S. General Accounting Office estimated that about 22 percent of all American workers have access to participation in a DCAP at their place of work.[8]

There are several limitations associated with DCAPs:

- Not all caregiving expenses are eligible for reimbursement, that is, only those expenses incurred as a result of an employee's working are eligible.
- Care must be provided by someone other than an employee's dependent (e.g., child or nonemployed spouse).[9]
- In order for care-related expenses to be reimbursed, receipts or invoices indicating the care provider's name, place of business, and Social Security or tax identification number must be submitted. This requirement effectively eliminates care provided by in-home care providers who are willing to earn less than the minimum wage to avoid reporting wages to the Internal Revenue Service.
- There is an annual limit on the dollars that can be set aside (currently $5,000).
- Dollars in the account will be of little or no use if the needed services are not available for purchase in the community in which the care recipient resides.
- Each year employees must specify, in advance of the start of the tax year, the amount that is to be deducted from their gross salary or wages; these dollars are forfeited if they are not spent by the end of the year.

This last limitation is, perhaps, the single most significant impediment to providing financial relief for some caregivers. Often, workers take on their new role as caregivers in crisis situations. As discussed in Chapter 2, denial of one's own aging and denial of the declining health of one's parents often mitigate against planning for elder care. This lack of planning often results in caregivers forfeiting the opportunity to gain some relief via the DCAP mechanism. See Appendix C for sources of additional information on the tax code and DCAPs.

Long-Term Care Insurance

In order to help people protect against the high cost of long-term care either in a nursing home or at home, the insurance industry began to offer long-term care insurance (LTCI) in the 1980s. Since neither Medicare, Medicare supplemental insurance, nor private health insurance are intended to cover chronic conditions or long-term care, especially custodial care (i.e., personal care that supplements or replaces a frail older person's self-care and does not require or entail trained or professional skills), LTCI policies were created to fill this gap.

A small but growing number of employers are offering long-term care insurance (LTCI) as an employee benefit. As of January 1997, about 1,000 employers offered LTCI.[10] Between 1987 and 1995, the total number of LTCI policies sold in the United States increased from 815,000 to 4.35 million, providing coverage for about 5 percent of eligible adults.[11] Federal legislation enacted in 1996 made major changes in the tax treatment of LTCI, patterning the tax status of LTCI premium costs after that of health coverage costs. By offering LTCI as a benefit, an employer encourages workers to plan for their future long-term care needs (and related costs). The employer may also offer to allow relatives of employees to purchase this insurance at the employer-negotiated group rates, thus providing a financial saving for employees' older relatives compared to what they would pay for comparable coverage under an individual policy.

Under the Health Insurance Portability and Accountability Act of 1996, LTCI policies effective January 1, 1997 are treated as accident and health insurance contracts with several favorable tax consequences. To be eligible for tax advantages, that is, in order to be tax-qualified, LTCI policies sold after January 1, 1997 must meet certain standards, including consumer protection standards as set forth in the Long Term Care Insurance Model Act and Model Regulations developed by the National Association of Insurance Commissioners.

As summarized by Feldesman, the tax benefits for qualified plans include the following:

- Subject to limitations in amount, a taxpayer may treat LTCI premiums as unreimbursed medical expenses and as such, deduct them from taxable income to the extent such expenses exceed 7.5 percent of the taxpayers adjusted gross income. The limits on deductions of annual premium dollars vary with the age of the insured.
- Employers may deduct premiums they pay for policies offered through employee benefit programs.
- Benefits received by taxpayers under a LTCI contract are excludable from gross income, subject to a cap of $175.00 per day. The dollar cap will be indexed for inflation according to the medical care cost component of the consumer price index.
- Employer-provided long-term care benefits are tax free to the employee. They are not excludable by an employee, however, if provided through a cafeteria plan of benefits.[12]

Subsidized Care and Vouchers

In order to reduce the number of unanticipated absences from work, some employers reimburse employees for a portion of the cost of emergency backup elder care. The employer may enter into a contract with a local vendor for a predetermined price per unit of service (e.g., one hour of time for a companion to stay with the elder) or may simply reimburse the eligible employee a flat amount per occurrence up to an annual dollar limit. Alternatively, the employer may issue vouchers redeemable for the stated amount at elder care providers who are included on a company-approved list. See the model program description at the end of this chapter for an example of an Emergency Back-Up Care Service that includes subsidized care.

SERVICES

Education

Employer-sponsored seminars and workshops can offer employees valuable information on such topics as the following:

- Elder care resources in the community.
- Basics of Medicare and Medicaid.
- How to select a home care agency, assisted living residence or nursing home.
- Legal issues and elder care.
- Family decision making.
- How to talk about money issues with your parent.
- Depression or dementia?: How to tell the difference.

Presenting such seminars in an easily accessible format (e.g., at the work site during lunch hour) can enhance attendance. Good sources of qualified speakers for such seminars include the local area agency on aging, hospital social services department, health and social service agencies (such as Visiting Nurse Associations or Family Service Agencies), college or university institutes on aging, and geriatric care managers.

The AARP *Caregivers in the Work Place Kit* provides step-by-step guidance for choosing seminar topics, using effective training methods, and evaluating results. See Appendix C, Resources for Managers.

Guidebooks and Video and Audio Tapes

The company library should include book titles relating to elder care issues, as well as a supply of current pamphlets, brochures, and consumer guides. Many of the latter are available free of charge from public and private organizations. See Appendix C for sources of such materials and a list of recommended book and videotape titles.

Guidebooks and Newsletters

A guidebook to elder care issues and resources can serve as a valuable first reference for three groups of employees: those who may want to learn more about elder care in general, in order to begin planning for a potential elder care situation in the future; those who are facing an elder care crisis and need a quick orientation to the basic issues and resources; and those who have been involved in an ongoing, perhaps long-term, elder caregiving relationship. A guidebook can provide a fresh perspective, confirm what they are doing right, or point the way to resources they may not have tapped.

Consulting firms specializing in work/family issues and vendors of elder care resource and referral services can offer such guides, often tailored to the needs of the organization. Also, see Appendix C, Resources for Caregivers, for examples of popular elder care guidebooks available in most book stores.

Specialized newsletters can reach working caregivers with valuable information to help them manage their own stresses and find the help they need for their aging relatives. Several organizations offer such publications as a membership service or on an annual subscription basis. See Appendix C, Resources for Caregivers for details.

Software Programs and Sites on the World Wide Web

The resources available from these sources changes rapidly and quality varies widely. Consult with one of the national groups concerned with caregiver issues to obtain an up to date list of worthwhile products and information sources.

Caregiver Fairs

This lunch time or before/after work program invites representatives of organizations serving elders to come to the work site, distribute literature, and answer questions. The objectives of the Caregivers Fair are to provide an opportunity for employees to familiarize themselves with community groups offering services to the elderly, provide an opportunity for employees to develop personal contacts with service providers without taking time away from work, and facilitate positive relationships among community groups and the employer.

By providing easy access to many kinds of elder care resources, the employer can help ease caregivers' difficult task of sifting through the maze of services available in a community. First developed by The Travelers Companies, the Caregivers Fair concept has been tested in many settings and found to be an effective way of assisting working caregivers. Keys factors in conducting a successful Caregivers Fair include the following:

- Begin planning well in advance; at least ten weeks of lead time is needed.
- Involve managers and other employees; participation in planning lays the groundwork for successful promotion and strong attendance on the day of the event.
- Begin publicizing the date, time, and location of the event well in advance; at least seven weeks prior to the date of the fair.
- Include a wide range of programs, services, and organizations; contact your local Area Agency on Aging (AAA) at the start of planning to obtain an overview of the range of key agencies that should be invited. The AAA maintains a comprehensive listing of elder services in its area.

- Send out invitations (see sample letter below) at least six weeks in advance of the event.
- Make follow-up phone calls to invited to organizations to confirm their attendance.
- Thank everyone involved in making the fair a success, inside and outside the company. A little recognition goes a long way toward assuring future cooperation.

Sample Invitation Letter from an Employer to Community Organizations for a Caregivers Fair

April 2, 199•

Dear (Name):

I am writing to invite (*name of organization*) to participate in a Caregivers Fair to take place from 12:00 noon to 2:30 p.m. on Wednesday, May 15 in the employee cafeteria located in the American Wonderworks corporate headquarters building at 111 Main Street, Waterbury, Connecticut.

Over half of all family caregivers caring for an older relative are employed. Research has shown that working caregivers experience a significant amount of stress in balancing their work and family responsibilities. American Wonderworks wants to support its employees who are concerned about or involved in caring for their older relatives. Our goal for the Caregivers Fair is to offer our employees information about organizations like yours, thus increasing employees' awareness of the supports available in the community.

We ask that you send a representative to the fair to answer questions from employees. In addition, please bring program literature for distribution. You will be assigned a table for display material and handouts. Promotional items are also welcome (e.g. tote bags, pens, key chains). Your space will be clearly marked, with a sign bearing your organization's name. We will provide set-up supplies and a hand truck for your use in carrying materials from the parking lot to the cafeteria.

A map detailing directions to our corporate headquarters is enclosed for your convenience. Please complete the brief registration form attached to the bottom of this letter and mail or fax it to (*name of contact*) at the above address or fax number. If you have any questions, please call me. We look forward to working with you to make this a valuable experience for our working caregivers.

Sincerely,

Name, Title

Please clip and return bottom portion by April 16:

Name of representatives attending fair:

Name of Organization:

Address:

Phone/Fax:

Contact person (if different from above):

Here are some other guidelines to follow:

* Address the letter to the executive director of the agency.
* Send the letter at least seven weeks in advance of the date of the Fair.
* Include a short response form and specify the desired response date.
* Designate someone to make follow up calls to each invitee if a response is not received by the date specified.

Resource and Referral

A resource and referral (R&R) service provides employees, and sometimes retirees, with personalized telephone and/or in-person consultation that includes information about services, information about possible providers of services in an older relative's community, assistance in formulating alternative plans of action, and assistance in finding needed information and services. This process may include referrals to professionals who can conduct an in-home assessment of the elder's needs, when appropriate.

A well-run R&R service can deliver results for the employer and for the working caregiver, including (1) reducing the amount of time spent on the telephone searching for and arranging elder care services; (2) reducing caregiver stress and increasing caregiver peace of mind by providing another set of objective "eyes and ears" to help sort out complex elder care situations; (3) reducing caregivers' tardiness and absences from work by focusing the search for appropriate housing and services, thus avoiding wasted time and effort; and (4) avoiding unnecessary levels of caregiver stress in the long run by exploring all the options available to the caregiver and the elder, thus increasing the likelihood of implementing an adaptable care plan that will work well over time.

IBM established the first national elder care R&R service in the 1980s, under contract with WFD, a work/life consulting firm. Following what today is a common pattern, IBM first offered a national child care R&R service, then expanded its offerings to include elder care. Today, there are at least three major national R&R vendors (see Appendix C, Resources for Managers) and dozens of local vendors.

Also known as consultation and referral (C&R) services, R&R is now a fairly common child care benefit offering among larger companies, with 36 percent offering this option of over 1,000 such employers according to one survey.[13] Elder care R&R is offered by about 26 percent of the same group. Among employers of all sizes, at least 7.7 million employees, or 8.3 percent of the American work force, have access through work to elder care R&R services. Almost 3 million of these workers have access to in-house (i.e., employer staff-provided) R&R, compared to 4.8 million who access R&R assistance via vendors who have contracts with their employers.[14]

In order to make a wise decision about inclusion of some form of R&R as a component of an employer's elder care offerings, the manager needs to understand the difference between corporate (i.e., employer-provided) R&R services and the information and referral services that are available to the general public through the federally-funded national aging network; and assess the pros and cons of engaging a local or national vendor of R&R services versus developing an internal elder care R&R capacity.

Public I&R Services: The Eldercare Locator

Basic information and referral (I&R) services for elder care are available free of charge to every American citizen via the national aging services network. Headquartered in Washington, D.C., the network's hub is the Administration on Aging (AoA), a division of the U.S. Department of Health and Human Services. In turn, each state operates a State Unit on Aging (SUA). Each SUA designates a local Area Agency on Aging (AAA) which operates an I&R service listing all elder care services in its designated area. Appendix A lists the addresses and phone numbers of all the SUAs and the AoA.

Thus, residents of any city or town in the United States may avail themselves of the information resources compiled for any other locality in the country. The AoA provides easy access to this network of information resources through a service known as the Eldercare Locator. Any resident of the United States can call the Eldercare Locator at (800) 677–1116 to obtain the phone number of the information and referral organization serving the area in which the older person in need of care resides. The local organization will then provide a list of providers offering the type(s) of elder services the caller is seeking. The quality and comprehensiveness of the resource listings varies, as does the quality of customer service at each local information and referral agency.

Corporate R&R Adds Assessment and Care Planning

For many people, gaining access to information about the availability of specific services does not solve their caregiving problems. Corporate R&R adds three dimensions or personal assistance to the services available through the publicly funded I&R network:

- Personalized assessment of the caregiver/care recipient situation.
- Personalized help in exploring the options available in order to develop a workable care plan.
- Personalized assistance in searching for and securing the information and services that the family needs in order to implement the care plan.

As explained in Chapter 3, the caregiver faces a six-step process in arranging for needed care. The first step is to accurately assess the total needs of the older care recipient. The second step is for the caregiver and the elder to assess the options available to them to meet the needs that have been identified. If the caregiver has accomplished these two initial tasks, then he or she is ready to begin making calls to inquire about the availability and cost of specific services to implement the care plan. In most cases, caregivers need assistance with the first and second steps before they begin their search. Often, they do not realize that they have omitted these important steps and they begin to search through the elder services maze to find services that will not actually produce a outcome that is satisfying to themselves or to the elder care recipient.

R&R services were developed to address this twofold problem. R&R services offer a single "800" telephone number to call where the working caregiver can speak to a trained elder care counselor. Using active listening techniques, the R&R counselor will assure that the caller examines the first two essential steps (assessing the elder's needs and exploring all options). R&R counselors report that the most common situation they encounter is the last-minute call from a stressed-out working caregiver whose frail older parent is experiencing an acute medical "crisis" (e.g., falling and fracturing a hip, or being hospitalized for another reason and then requiring an unprecedented level of physical assistance in order to regain normal day-to-day functioning). In such situations, the first reaction of the overwhelmed caregiver is to ask the R&R counselor for a list of "good" nursing homes in their parents' area. After carefully listening to the situation as described by the working caregiver, the counselor is often able to introduce options that the family has not considered because of lack of awareness of available services. Often, the counselor can help develop a plan that maximizes the elder's level of independent functioning at home or in a residential environment other than a nursing home.

Selecting an R&R Service Option

Most national R&R vendors charge an annual per capita fee for the service, adjusted according to the average age of the customer firm's work force and other factors. Depending on actual utilization over the course of the first year or two, the fee may be adjusted upward or downward. Most local R&R vendors (and some national firms) will offer the option of entering into contracts on a fee-for-service basis, that is, charging an agreed-upon flat fee for each call handled.

The needs of long distance caregivers are an important consideration in planning for an elder care R&R component. As noted in Chapter 3, the characteristics and needs of this group differ significantly from caregivers in general. Even among small groups of employees, the likelihood is high that some working caregivers will be assisting relatives who live at a distance. This means that any R&R offering needs to include the capability to competently and efficiently access needed information and services in other parts of the country.

The manager should consider the following pros and cons when assessing whether (or how) to offer an elder care R&R service:

1. **Employer staff model—Pros**
   - Control over quality of interaction with employees
   - Tailored service to match the particular needs of an organization's work force
   - Highly personalized service offers potential for effective links to local service network

2. **Employer staff model—Cons**
   - Potential employee reluctance to use service due to concerns about confidentiality of personal information
   - Relatively high cost per user if the annual service volume is not high
   - Limited capacity to collect, maintain, and access service information on a national basis
   - Potential liability exposure for employer related to consultation provided to employees

3. **Contracting with a national R&R vendor—Pros**
   - Potentially comprehensive national elder care database
   - Capability to track trends and deliver reports on utilization
   - Provision of high quality collateral materials (i.e., guidebooks, fact sheets)
   - May offer "self-serve" options for caregiver to conduct searches via the Internet or intranet
   - For large employers with dispersed work force and many long distance caregivers, assures availability of standard service at all locations
   - For larger employers, offers a cost effective alternative to developing internal capacity with lower liability exposure

4. **Contracting with a national R&R vendor—Cons**
   - For smaller employers, cost may be prohibitive
   - For larger employers with very low utilization, may not be cost effective
   - Depending on the service delivery model the vendor employs, may not deliver the personalized level of service the employer or caregiver desires

5. **Contracting with a local R&R vendor—Pros**
   - For smaller employers, as-used, fee-for-service pricing makes financial sense
   - Lower cost because of lower overhead
   - Even without a computerized database, an *experienced and skilled* elder care counselor can effectively access needed information and services in other cities
   - If the employer's work force is concentrated in one locale, a local vendor may be able to offer superior knowledge of local resources
   - Potentially more personalized approach, that is, the same staff who answers the R&R phone call may also conduct seminars on site or attend company sponsored caregiver fairs

6. Contracting with a local R&R vendor—Cons

- Unlikely to offer the comprehensive, continuously updated elder care data bases that the national vendors maintain, therefore more limited in effectiveness for long distance caregiving
- May lack depth of staff because of relatively low volume
- Potential lack of availability of quality collateral materials and management training capacity

Counseling

Historically, the counseling services provided by Employee Assistance Programs (EAPs) represented the first organized response to work/life balance concerns. Some employers began to offer EAP services as early as the 1950s. Initially, EAPs focused on providing counseling and other supports for employees with problems related to alcohol abuse. Most EAPs expanded to include substance abuse, psychological, and family counseling, among other services. Today, many have diversified to include elder care and child care related services, either directly or under subcontract arrangements with R&R vendors. Eighty-four percent of large employers offer EAPs.[15]

In regard to elder care program development, the manager should consider the following EAP-related questions. If the employer currently operates an EAP program,

- Do the counselors receive a significant number of elder-care related referrals?
- Does the EAP employ family therapy techniques (indicating a capacity to assist working caregivers with elder care situations)?
- Does the EAP offer an elder care R&R service directly or under contract?
- If the EAP does not offer an elder care R&R service, how would the EAP and a potential new R&R vendor assure coordination and complementarity of roles?
- Does the EAP employ any counselors who are specially trained in gerontology or geriatrics?

If the employer does not currently offer an EAP program and is considering offering one,

- Is there an EAP in the area that offers a comprehensive approach, that is, integrating traditional areas of EAP expertise with an elder care R&R capacity?
- What reputation does the EAP have among elder care specialists in the locations where most of the employer's work force is located?
- Does the EAP employ any counselors who are specially trained in gerontology or geriatrics?
- What links does the EAP have to mental health or health care resources for elders?

Geriatric Care Management

A growing number of professionals are offering private case or care management services designed to help caregivers locate and coordinate housing and services for older relatives. This service is particularly useful to long distance caregivers. In such situations, the geriatric care manager (GCM) may function as a gerontologically knowledgeable surrogate son or daughter. A handful of employers currently pay for all or part of the cost of a GCM's service. See the corporate profile of the Fel-Pro program at the end of this chapter for a case example.

A GCM provides a level of assistance which goes several steps beyond what is usually offered by an R&R vendor. A competent R&R vendor will maintain a listing of qualified GCMs throughout the country, and R&R counselors will refer working caregivers to GCMs when the situation warrants additional help.

Typically, the geriatric care manager will start by evaluating the elder's situation. This usually involves a visit to the elder's home or other place of residence. Next, the GCM will make recommendations and arrange appropriate services, keeping family members informed. Depending on circumstances, the family or elder may choose to engage the services of the GCM to monitor the implementation of the care plan and provide advice and assistance to modify arrangements, as needed.

GCM fees are usually structured to include a standard, one-time assessment charge, plus hourly charges for time incurred in arranging and monitoring services.

Private GCM services are frequently listed in the yellow pages under Social Services, Social Workers, Aging Services, Senior Citizen Services, and Home Health Care Organizations. The field is relatively new and most GCM providers are not regulated or licensed. Common backgrounds for GCMs include social work, nursing, and social service management related to elder care. The National Association of Geriatric Care Managers is developing an accreditation program for this specialty. See Appendix C, Resources for Caregivers, for further information.

On-Site Adult Day Care

An adult day center is a multipurpose program for physically frail or cognitively impaired older persons living in the community. Such a center will usually provide, on a daily basis, recreation and social services, hot meals, and, depending on the target population the center intends to serve, medical, nursing, and rehabilitation services. Adult day centers sometimes provide transportation to their location. Programs which include medical services are commonly referred to as adult day health services and are usually licensed by a state's department of public health.

Adult day centers offer an important support option for those working caregivers whose elder relatives cannot safely remain at home during the day. The center provides a safe, stimulating environment for the elder and can make it possible for some caregivers to maintain their jobs while avoiding nursing home placement for a frail older relative.

On-site or near-site child care centers are offered by about 8 percent of large employers.[16] A handful of employers have experimented with offering adult day health services for older relatives of employees. See Appendix C, Resources for Caregivers, for sources of information on starting and managing an adult day center.

Caregiver Support Groups

Caregiver support groups can serve as a valuable source of emotional support and practical problem solving ideas and techniques. A support group is formed by extending an invitation to employees with similar kinds of dependent care concerns to meet on a regular basis. The group discussion sessions are facilitated by a professional (e.g., a social worker, psychologist, or geriatric nurse practitioner). About 5 million workers are employed by organizations that provide access to participation in elder caregiver support groups.[17]

Support groups can be organized by an employer's own staff, by the EAP program, a community agency, or by an elder care R&R vendor. In some cases, the employer may wish to inform employees of existing support groups that meet in the community. Conducting caregiver support group meetings on site is a viable option, but timing is important. Participants in on-site groups report that, following participation in a emotionally draining group discussion, it is difficult to return to work and focus on work tasks. Therefore, such sessions should be scheduled at the end of the work day or after regular work hours.

In the community, such groups are organized by, for example, the local chapters of Alzheimers Disease and Related Disorders Association and the Easter Seal Society, which operates "stroke clubs" that help stroke victims and their family members adapt to life after a stroke. See Appendix C, Resources for Caregivers, for sources of information on organizing support groups.

Resource Development

As mentioned earlier in this chapter, an employer can play an important role in developing services to fill gaps in the availability of needed elder care. On the national level, the American Business Collaboration for Quality Dependent Care, established in 1992, has channeled funding from major corporations to increase the supply and quality of dependent care services in the United States. Though most of the funding has supported child care service development, the collaboration has supported such elder care initiatives as adult day care, Alzheimer's Safe Return, and Meals on Wheels service expansion and leadership development.

WFD, the consulting firm that manages the effort, reports that during phase one (1992 to 1995) the Collaborative invested $27.4 million in 355 dependent care projects serving forty-five targeted communities.[18] For phase two (1995 to 2000) the CEOs of twenty-two leading corporations participating in the collaboration have committed to investing $100 million for the development of projects in more than sixty targeted communities. The twenty-two "Champion Companies" include Aetna, Allstate Insurance Co., American Express, Amoco, AT&T, Bank of America, Citibank, Chevron, Deloitte & Touche, Eastman Kodak, Exxon, GE Capital Services, Hewlett-Packard, IBM, Johnson & Johnson, Lucent Technologies, Mobil, NYNEX (Bell Atlantic), Price Waterhouse, Texaco, Texas Instruments, and Xerox.

For an example of a successful local program with expanded resources for elder care and child care, see the Kids' Line Phone Pals model program description at the end of this chapter.

CORPORATE PROFILES

The corporate profiles presented below describe the different paths taken by Digital Equipment Company, the computer hardware and software firm, and Fel-Pro, Inc., an automotive parts manufacturer, as they developed the elder care components of their work/life initiatives.

Digital Equipment Company

After Restructuring: Work/Life Survives and Expands Into Elder Care
Corporate Headquarters: Maynard, Massachusetts
Number of Employees in 1997: approximately 25,000 (U.S.); 55,000 (worldwide)

Like many other large firms, Digital Equipment Company underwent tremendous changes in the size and organization of its work force during the 1990s. Before the downsizing that began in 1991, Digital employed 125,000 people worldwide. In 1997, the company employed about 55,000 people. In the United States, the total shrunk from 73,000 to under 25,000. Yet, the core of its work/family effort survived. In the mid-1990s, the company began reshaping its effort to adapt to its new economic and employment environment.

Digital's involvement with work/family programs began in the late 1980s with child care. The program progressed in a manner which parallels the growth and evolution of the work/life field itself. Elder care was always a part of the agenda. The commitment to developing an elder care component of the work/life program grew out of a research effort conducted in cooperation with Boston University's Center for Work and Family in the 1980s. The research results showed that although elder care was an issue for some workers at that time, it would become a much bigger concern over the next five years.

Then, Digital entered its period of economic crisis. In the early 1990s, aggressive restructuring precluded bringing on new work/life programs. However, existing work/life initiatives were maintained with some enhancements.

In late 1994, the work/life manager presented a formal proposal for introduction of an elder care program. Digital began offering a consultation and referral service for working caregivers under contract with a national vendor, along with psychological support provided by its EAP program. Policies include a wide range of tools allowing for flexible work arrangements. The use of those tools is at the discretion of its managers.

The new elder care offering coincided with a rebranding of the entire work/family and EAP effort. The new program merged the direct services which were previously provided under the separate headings of Employee Assistance and Family Resource Services. In addition, the company reevaluated how it was communicating these offerings, focusing on how the employee, the end user of the services, was receiving the messages being communicated. The objective was to structure a program that took advantage of the most efficient, clearest way of communicating.

Running a parallel course, Digital benefits strategies, as well as its work/life programs, began to adopt a lifecycle point of view, emphasizing a continuum of care, that is, an approach that included a broad range of offerings that addressed the changing needs of employees over time. Digital named the initiative *Work/Life Connections*^{SM}.

The aftereffects of restructuring have included major changes in the company's culture and environment. For example, the focus of human resources activities has shifted to reengaging employees and redefining the partnership with employees. This involves working out questions such as: What does the company give? What do employees give? What do the two parties give to each other?

As part of the process of employee reengagement, Digital began to refocus on work/life balance issues. In the past, planning focused on the development of specific programs, like elder care. Now, the company has begun to look at work/life issues in a broader, more comprehensive context. This review includes, for example, attention to behaviors and practices of managers in regard to allowing employees the flexibility they need to fulfill their obligations in caring for older relatives. The effort will also consider the constant shifts and movements in technology as well as the kinds of employee talents needed to stay ahead of competitors.

Digital's *WorkLife Connections* effort also seeks to incorporate the perspective of younger employees—those in their twenties and thirties. These newer members of Digital's work force bring a different set of value issues to their work, expressing a strong desire to find a healthier work/life balance.

Work/life program manager Bruce Davidson has worked at Digital through all the changes of the 1980s and 1990s. He summed up his view of the experience in this way: "My basic message to line managers is (1) Respect for the employee is an underpinning across the board, and (2) You have got to focus on issues of flexibility. The key is to build relationships with employees that allow for negotiation and discussion about what the person's personal needs are, and what the business needs are. Productivity and success are built off coming up with compromises and plans that are needed by those two entities. If the relationship is built on an attitude that says: 'This is what I need. I don't care what's going on in your life' that creates a point where employees are caught in a bind between their need for the job and their need to meet their personal responsibility for care of their elders. It creates the inherent conflict in the employees' attempts to balance work and family life. Research data indicate that either people get sick or there are increased somatic complaints, increased stress, potential for disability. Sometimes, the person quits and looks for another job that provides the needed flexibility. It's an untenable conflict that the employer/supervisor places on the employee.

"Different industries have different needs. In some cases, turnover may not be as much of an issue as it is in the computer field. In this industry, the talents of certain employees are regarded as less expendable and the costs related to turnover are high. Work/family balance for working caregivers and others takes a higher strategic priority in an environment where employers need to retain talent and limit involuntary turnover. The work environment needs to provide the kind of help these employees need."

Fel-Pro, Inc.

Elder Care Benefits in Transition: Care Management
Corporate Headquarters: Skokie, Illinois
Manufacturer of automotive parts (gaskets, lubricants, and sealants)
Number of Employees, 1997: 3,000 (2,500 in the United States)

Fel-Pro is an unusual company. It employs a relatively small work force in a manufacturing environment, and it has successfully integrated a wide range of family-friendly benefits into its operations. Surrounded by and doing business with the unionized facilities of the big three American auto manufacturers, Fel-Pro maintains a nonunion work force. It is one of the few organizations of its size that employs a full-time manager to oversee its work/life program. When President Clinton signed into law the Family and Medical Leave Act of 1993, Fel-Pro President Paul Lehman stood at his side, the only business executive present that day.

Scott Mies, Fel-Pro's director of work/life benefits, explains the company's commitment in historical terms: "We have an 80-year tradition, a basic philosophy that says 'If you treat your employees well and you care about them,

they will work hard for you and you will be a successful company.' We realize that employees do bring their home problems to work and they take their
work problems home. And if you deny that or pretend that that is not the case,
then you're just treading water because people are preoccupied at work with
child care issues, elder care issues, legal issues, social issues. Many different
things can preoccupy them or cause a lack of productivity. We try to go down
the list categorically and look at each one of those needs and see how we can
make it easier for them."

The comprehensive work/life balance benefits plan at the company today
has its roots in the earliest days of Fel-Pro's operations. The family owners
took a personal interest in their employees, an interest that today some might
call paternalistic. They would walk through the plant each morning, greeting
and talking with the employees, getting to know their families, and organizing company-sponsored family gatherings.

Fel-Pro has gone well beyond company picnics in creating a family atmosphere. In the early 1950s, Fel-Pro instituted an employee forum to give its
workers a voice. Employees elected delegates from various areas of the company and brought forward issues, grievance, compliments, and complaints
for management's attention. The company's 220 acre recreation facility for
employees opened twenty-five years ago. Work/life initiatives began in the
1970s with a progressive family leave policy.

In 1977, Fel-Pro entered into an arrangement with a local organization to
provide a resource and referral consultation service for its employees caring
for older relatives, including publication of a bimonthly elder care newsletter. It was one of the first companies in the country to incorporate such an
elder care service in its benefit package. Representatives of the local group
with which Fel-Pro contracted set up an elder care resource table in the employee cafeteria on a regular basis in order to provide ongoing information
and communication. In 1983, Fel-Pro opened its on-site child care center
which today incorporates an intergenerational approach: A small number of
Fel-Pro retirees volunteer their time with the children under the supervision
of the center's professional staff.

The average age of the Fel-Pro's work force is forty-one, well above the national norm. Consequently, elder care has emerged as an important area for the
company's attention. In 1996, the company examined its elder care offerings and
decided, based on feedback from employees who used the R&R service, that
the approach did not fully address employee concerns as effectively as needed.

As part of the evaluation process, work/life benefits director Mies took the
time to more fully educate himself about the dynamics of elder care. "I began
to realize that, with our resource and referral service, we were only dealing
with the outer layers of the onion. There were much deeper layers that we
hadn't uncovered, like really walking our working caregivers through the
process." He cited a conversation with a female employee who had used the
R&R service. She explained how the service had treated her very nicely, lis-

tened very well to her situation, and, after exploring options on the phone with her, had provided her with a list of several affordable residential facilities which could meet her frail father's needs, along with a checklist she could use to evaluate them and make a choice. "I could tell by the tone of her voice that something was wrong," said Mies. "I don't know," she said to Mies, "Calling all these places . . . I don't really know what to look for. I don't have time to do this. I can't do this." She burst into tears on the phone. "Don't you understand, emotionally I *can't* do this," she said. "I need someone to do this with me." Mies cited this experience as helping him realize that what some working caregivers needed was someone who would go beyond researching and presenting information on services options.

In 1997, Fel-Pro engaged a local firm, staffed by geriatrically trained nurses that will offer direct geriatric care management services beginning in 1998. In order to build a personal rapport with employees, the same staff person from the service tends to the monthly caregiver information table in the cafeteria. The company will pay a flat fee for a personalized in-home assessment of the elder's needs, when appropriate, and development of a care plan to address a working caregiver's individual family needs. The service includes "taking the employee by the hand," as Mies puts it, connecting the family to the specific service provider or providers who can solve the identified problem. For an employee whose elder relative lives in a distant part of the country, the contract agency has established arrangements with geriatric care managers around the country who will deliver a comparable service in other cities. Fel-Pro uses the service on a pay-as-you-go basis, operating within an annual cap on potential reimbursement.

A limited flextime approach enhances Fel-Pro's elder care supports. "We are a hard-core manufacturing company," says Mies. "Compared to a white collar, office-type environment, it is much more difficult to offer individual flextime options. We operate on a team-based approach with people on assembly lines, operating punch presses, etc." The company does allow for flexible starting and stopping times that are agreed upon by the individual teams. For example, a team can vote to work from 7:00 to 3:30 instead of the standard 9:00 to 5:00 in order to accommodate the needs of team members to best meet their family schedules. Because of the nature of the work performed, few Fel-Pro employees can avail themselves of options like telecommuting or job-sharing which are more commonly offered in an office environment.

MODEL PROGRAM DESCRIPTIONS

Emergency Back-Up Care Service

Employer: Harvard University
Contact: Manager, Office of Work and Family
Location: Cambridge, Massachusetts

Program Description: Back-up care includes in-home adult companion care or child care provided on short notice so the employee can come to work when regular arrangements for care fall through due to an ill or absent caregiver, snow days, a mildly ill child, or other temporary circumstances. The university pays an annual corporate membership fee to a local vendor which then provides this service to eligible employees at a reduced corporate rate (about 50 percent of what an individual member of the vendor's program would pay). Eligible employees may use up to fifty hours of subsidized care per year. Adult care services include reading, walking with the elder, and light meal preparation. Hands-on care is not provided, although the vendor can provide such care for an additional hourly rate paid directly by the employee.

How It Works: Eligible employees (those working over 17.5 hours per week) must preregister at least one week in advance of first using the service. The employee calls the vendor directly when service is needed and is directly billed for services used, at the corporate rate. The employee also pays all transportation costs for the companion. The vendor requests a twenty-four-hour notice. Service must be purchased for a minimum of three hours per day.

Caregiver Information Model

Employer: Social Security Administration (SSA)
Location: Baltimore, Maryland
Contact: Manager, Dependent Care Programs
The Baltimore office of the Social Security Program developed an elder care initiative for its own employees with three purposes in mind: (1) to help employees recognize that they are or may soon be a caregiver, (2) to inform employees about the issues involved in caregiving, and (3) to put employees in contact with community resources that can help employees with their caregiving responsibilities.

The program operates on the premise that providing accurate, timely information about caregiving issues and services allows working caregivers to better anticipate difficulties, making the caregiving experience less stressful and thus reducing losses in productivity. Two-thirds of the 14,000 workers at the Social Security headquarters are women, with an average age of forty-five years. With this profile, it was obvious to program planner Tom Pugh that elder care deserved a high priority.

The program accomplishes its purposes by conducting a variety of informational activities on an ongoing basis. The emphasis is on preventing disruptions in work and productivity by bringing needed information to working caregivers before they experience a crisis situation. Since its inception in 1992, activities have included the following:

• Regular broadcasts of programs on elder care issues on the SSA National Satellite Network presented by professional experts in the elder care field, viewed at forty-five local offices. Broadcasts have included topics such as making homes senior-friendly, getting legal affairs in order, coping with death and dying, new outlook on aging, and an introduction to senior living arrangements. Speakers are obtained free of charge through referrals at local community agencies.

- Videotapes of the broadcasts are made available for employee viewing on a rental basis through the local Career Life Resource Center.
- Free program information and brochures from public and private agencies are distributed.
- Annual Caregiver Fair is held on-site.
- Caregiver support groups are conducted on-site, with facilitators provided by local family services agencies.

Kids' Line Phone Pals: An Intergenerational Approach

Employer: Bell Atlantic
Unions: Communications Workers of America (CWA) and the International Brotherhood of Electrical Workers (IBEW)
Location: Pittsburgh, Pennsylvania
Contact: Executive Director, Contact, Inc., Pittsburgh

A group of homebound older volunteers in the Pittsburgh area handle 12,000 calls a year from latchkey children of Bell Atlantic employees. The elders look forward to receiving the calls as much as the children enjoy talking to their Kids' Line grandmothers and grandfathers. Thanks to the efforts of the elders, Bell Atlantic employees can finish up their workday activities with a little more peace of mind, knowing that someone who cares is checking in on their sons and daughters.

In 1993, the executive director of the Vintage senior center in Pittsburgh heard that Bell Atlantic was seeking to work with a local agency that could help address a work/life balance issue of concern to members of the two unions at the company. Workers were anxious about their children remaining alone between the time the children arrived home from school and the time parents returned from work. The senior center collaborated with Contact, Inc., a crisis intervention telephone hotline service, to set up a central "800" number that the children could call. When the phone rings at the Contact center, it is immediately routed to one of the carefully screened and trained older persons who have volunteered to help.

Funding for the service comes from a special fund that was established as a component of the collective bargaining agreements between Bell Atlantic and CWA and IBEW and Bell Atlantic. The purpose of the fund is to increase the supply of dependent care services that will help union members better balance their work and family lives. Ceridian Performance Partners administers the fund for Bell Atlantic in accord with funding priorities set by CWA's Advisory Council on Family Care and the IBEW's Advisory Committee on Career and Life Strategies. The annual operating budget is in the range of

$60,000 to $70,000. In addition to the cost of the telephone calls (some of which originate in other mid-Atlantic states, as well as the Pittsburgh area), the program budget includes the cost of back-up staffing. Contact staff support the volunteers and the agency operates an automated service to cover the phones after hours and on weekends because some of the children call at those times as well. The program is modeled after a similar project called Grandma, Please, developed at Hull House, a settlement house in Chicago.

As word of the program's success spread in the community, Kids' Line Phone Pals has stimulated the development of other elder care resources. A collaborative effort involving the local Interfaith Caregivers group has mobilized volunteers to provide telephone reassurance, snow shoveling help, and other services for homebound elders in the Pittsburgh area. The CWA/IBEW dependent care resource fund has provided seed money for these programs as well.

THE FUTURE OF ELDER CARE AND WORK

The worldwide phenomenon of an aging population and the decreasing availability of younger family members to care for the growing number of elders will radically transform social institutions, business enterprises, and the very fabric of everyday life in the twenty-first century. Over the next ten years, the use of employee benefits for working caregivers will dramatically increase, and work/life balance will emerge as an important strategic business issue, as well as a top item on the nation's political agenda. The full impact of caregiving demands on the aging of the baby boom generation will be felt beginning in 2000 and will increase steadily through 2020. As the baby boomers pass through their fifties and sixties, they will make their need for increased help with elder caregiving a major issue for employers and for public policy makers. Industries which rely on knowledge for continued growth and development will need to include effective elder care responses as part of their work/life cycle program offerings in order to remain competitive.

Increased mobility among employees will mean more workers with long distance caregiving needs. As companies, especially larger ones, continue to consolidate workers into megacenters and eliminate layers of middle management, more workers will leave behind the towns where they were born and raised. When they move, they will also leave their parents behind. Consequently, the number of family caregivers who live in close proximity to their aging parents will continue to dwindle. Some baby boomers will convince their frail, older relatives to move with them, but not necessarily to move in with them. This minitrend will drive the continued growth in the number of upscale assisted living residences because these offer a pleasant, safe environment for the elder as well as peace of mind for the adult children.

Employee mobility and retrenchment in public funding will increase demand for private-pay home care help and for geriatric care management. The latter service is likely to rise in popularity as an employee benefit because it offers an effective way to reduce distraction and cut time losses related to finding and arranging elder care from a distance.

Working caregivers will benefit from a gradual rationalization of the currently fragmented, nonsystem of long-term care for the elderly and disabled. Managed care plans will adapt their offerings to meet new customer demands to better address the needs of both working caregivers and their parents. The transformation of hospital networks into integrated delivery systems will continue, with a net decline in the number of acute care beds and an increase in home and community care services designed to cost-effectively care for the growing numbers of frail older people. Medicare and Medicaid will enter into direct contracts with these systems for the delivery of the full continuum of long-term care services. Employers will begin to insist on closer cooperation among the separate divisions of managed care plans that serve the Medicare population and the younger, employed population.

Other specific changes in the needs of working caregivers and in elder care benefits offerings will include increased use of "self-service" approaches to elder care service arrangements, especially via employers' intranets and the Internet, increased enrollment in long-term care insurance plans offered by employers as baby boomers in the middle income group realize the need to protect their assets from the future ravages of long-term care expenses, and increased attention to caregiver stress management through managed care plans.

NOTES

1. Barney Olmsted and Suzanne Smith, *Managing in a Flexible Workplace* (New York: AMACOM, 1997), 21–189.

2. The Conference Board, *Work–Family Roundtable: Part-Time Employment* (New York: The Conference Board, 1996).

3. Katherine Esty, Richard Griffin, and Marcie Schorr Hirsch, *Workplace Diversity: A Manager's Guide to Solving Problems and Turning Diversity into a Competitive Advantage* (Holbrook, Mass.: Adams Media, 1995), 3.

4. Margaret B. Neal, Nancy J. Chapman, Berit Ingersoll-Dayton, and Arthur C. Emlen, *Balancing Work and Caregiving for Children, Adults, and Elders* (Newbury Park, Calif.: Sage Publications, 1993), 210.

5. M. Z. Goldstein, ed., *Family Involvement in the Treatment of the Frail Elderly* (Washington, D.C.: American Psychiatric Press, 1988), 157–201.

6. Neal et al., *Balancing Work and Caregiving*, 211.

7. M. J. Canan and W. D. Mitchell, *Employee Fringe and Welfare Benefit Plans* (St. Paul, Minn.: West Publishers, 1991).

8. U.S. General Accounting Office (GAO), *Long Term Care: Public Sector Elder Care Could Yield Multiple Benefits* (Washington, D.C.: U.S. General Accounting Office, 1994), 7.

9. A. E. Scharlach, B. F. Lowe, and E. L. Schneider, *Elder Care and the Work Force: Blueprint for Action* (Lexington, Mass.: D. C. Heath and Company, 1991).

10. Danae A. Manus, "Why Bother with Long-Term Care Coverage?," *Business and Health* (January 1997): 23–27.

11. David Bryce and Yoshiko Yarnada, "Facts on Long Term Care," *Gerontology News* (September 1997): 7–8.

12. Walter Feldesman, *Dictionary of Eldercare Terminology* (Washington, D.C.: United Seniors Health Cooperative, 1997), 118–119.

13. Marie Lipari and Saline Leckman, *Work and Family Benefits Provided by Major U.S. Employers in 1996* (Lincolnshire, Ill.: Hewitt Associates, LLC, 1997), 1.

14. GAO, *Long Term Care*, 7.

15. Lipari and Leckman, *Work and Family Benefits*, 1.

16. Ibid., 3.

17. GAO, *Long Term Care*, 7.

18. WFD, "CEO's Statement on The American Business Collaboration for Quality Dependent Care," *Fact Sheet*, 14 September 1995.

Appendix A

State Units on Aging

Alabama
Commission on Aging
RSA Plaza, Suite 470
770 Washington Ave.
Montgomery, AL 36130
334–242–5743
Fax: 334–242–5594

Alaska
Division of Senior Services
Department of Administration
3601 C St., #310
Anchorage, AK 99503
907–563–5654
Fax: 907–562–3040

Arizona
Aging and Adult Administration
Department of Economic Security
1789 W. Jefferson, #950A
Phoenix, AZ 85007
602–542–4446
Fax: 602–542–6575

Arkansas
Division of Aging and Adult Services
Arkansas Dept. of Human Services
P.O. Box 1437, Slot 1412
7th and Main Streets
Little Rock, AR 72201
501–682–2441
Fax: 501–682–8155

California
Department of Aging
1600 K Street
Sacramento, CA 95814
916–322–5290
Fax: 916–324–1903

Colorado
Division of Aging and Adult Services
Dept. of Human Services
110 16th Street, #200
Denver, CO 80202–5202
303–620–4147
Fax: 303–620–4189

Connecticut
Department of Social Services
Elderly Services Division
25 Sigourney St., 10th floor
Hartford, CT 06106–5033
860–424–5277
Fax: 860–424–4966

Delaware
Division of Services for Aging & Adults
  with Physical Disabilities
Dept. of Health and Social Services
1901 North Dupont Highway
New Castle, DE 19720
302–577–4791
Fax: 302–577–4793

District of Columbia
Office on Aging
One Judiciary Square
441 4th Street, N.W., 9th floor
Washington, DC 20001
202–724–5622
Fax: 202–724–4979

Florida
Department of Elder Affairs
Building B, Suite 152
4040 Esplanade Way
Tallahassee, FL 32399
904–414–2000
Fax: 904–414–2002

Georgia
Office on Aging
#2 Peachtree St. N.E., 18th floor
Atlanta, GA 30303
404–657–5258
Fax: 404–657–5285

Guam
Division of Senior Citizens
Dept. of Public Health and Social Services
Government of Guam
P.O. Box 2816
Agana, Guam 96910
011–671–475–0263
Fax: 011–671–477–2930

Hawaii
Executive Office on Aging
No. 1 Capitol District
250 South Hotel St., Suite 107
Honolulu, HI 96813–2831
808–586–0100
Fax: 808–586–0185

Idaho
Commission on Aging
700 W. Jefferson, Room 108
P.O. Box 7, Boise, ID 83720–0007
208–334–2423
Fax: 208–334–3033

Illinois
Dept. on Aging
421 East Capitol Ave.
Springfield, IL 62701
217–785–2870
Fax: 217–785–4477

Indiana
Bureau of Aging/In-Home Services
402 West Washington St., #E-431
Indianapolis, IN 46207–7083
317–232–7020
Fax: 317–232–7867

Iowa
Dept. of Elder Affairs
Clemens Bldg., 3rd floor
200 Tenth St.
Des Moines, IA 50309–3609
515–281–5187
Fax: 515–281–4036

Kansas
Dept. on Aging
Docking State Office Bldg., 122-S
915 S.W. Harrison
Topeka, KS 66612–1500
913–296–4986
Fax: 913–296–0256

Kentucky
Division of Aging Services
Cabinet for Human Resources

275 East Main Street, 6 West
Frankfort, KY 40621
502–564–6930
Fax: 502–564–4595

Louisiana
Office of Elderly Affairs
P.O. Box 80374
412 N. 4th St.
Baton Rouge, LA 70802
504–342–7100
Fax: 504–342–7133

Maine
Bureau of Elder and Adult Services
State House, Station #11
Augusta, ME 04333
207–624–5335
Fax: 207–624–5361

Mariana Islands
CNMI Office on Aging, DC&CA
P.O. Box 2178
Saipan, MP 96950
011–671–734–4361
Fax: 011–671–477–2930

Maryland
Office on Aging
State Office Bldg., Room 1004
301 West Preston St.
Baltimore, MD 21201
410–767–1100
Fax: 410–333–7943

Massachusetts
Executive Office of Elder Affairs
One Ashburton Place, 5th floor
Boston, MA 02108
617–222–7434
Fax: 617–727–6944

Michigan
Office of Services to the Aging
P.O. Box 30676
Lansing, MI 48909–8176
517–373–8230
Fax: 517–373–4092

Minnesota
Board on Aging
444 Lafayette Rd.
St. Paul, MN 55155–3843
612–296–2770
Fax: 612–297–7855

Mississippi
Council on Aging
Division of Aging
   and Adult Services
750 N. State St.
Jackson, MS 39202
601–359–4929
Fax: 601–359–4370

Missouri
Division on Aging
Dept. of Social Services
P.O. Box 1337
615 Howerton Court
Jefferson City, MO 65102–1337
573–751–3082
Fax: 573–751–8687

Montana
Senior Long Term Care Division
111 Sanders St.
P.O. Box 4210
Helena, MT 59604
406–444–7743
Fax: 406–444–7743

Nebraska
Division on Aging
P.O. Box 95044
301 Centennial Mall-South
Lincoln, NE 68509
402–471–2306
Fax: 402–471–2306

Nevada
Division for Aging Services
Dept. of Human Resources
340 N. 11th St., Suite 203
Las Vegas, NV 89101
702–486–3545
Fax: 702–486–3572

New Hampshire
Division of Elderly and Adult Services
State Office Park South
115 Pleasant St., Annex Bldg. #1
Concord, NH 03301–3843
603–271–4680
Fax: 603–271–4643

New Jersey
Division of Senior Affairs
Department of Health & Senior
  Services
CN 807
South Broad and Front Streets
Trenton, NJ 08625–0807
609–292–3766; 800–792–8820
Fax: 609–633–6609

New Mexico
State Agency on Aging
La Villa Rivera Bldg.
224 East Palace Ave., 4th floor
Santa Fe, NM 87501
505–827–7640
Fax: 505–827–7649

New York
Office for the Aging
New York State Plaza, Agency Bldg. #2
Albany, NY 12223
518–474–4425
Fax: 518–474–1398

North Carolina
Division on Aging
CB 29531
693 Palmer Drive
Raleigh, NC 27626–0531
919–733–3983
Fax: 919–733–0443

North Dakota
Aging Services Division
Dept. of Human Services
600 South 2nd St., Suite 1C
Bismark, ND 58504
701–328–8909
Fax: 701–328–8989

Ohio
Department of Aging
50 West Broad St., 9th floor
Columbus, OH 43215–5928
614–466–5500
Fax: 614–466–5741

Republic of Palau
Agency on Aging
P.O. Box 100
Koror, PW 96940

Rhode Island
Dept. of Elderly Affairs
160 Pine St.
Providence, RI 02903–3708
401–277–2858
Fax: 401–277–1490

(American) Samoa
Territorial Administration on Aging
American Samoan Government
Pago Pago, American Samoa 96799
011–684–633–1252

South Carolina
Division on Aging
Office of the Governor, 1801 Main St.
Columbia, SC 29202
803–253–6177
Fax: 803–253–4173

South Dakota
Office of Adult Services and Aging
700 Governors Drive
Pierre, SD 57501
605–773–3656
Fax: 605–773–4855

Tennessee
Commission on Aging
Andrew Jackson Bldg.
500 Deaderick Bldg., 9th floor
Nashville, TN 37243–0860
615–741–2056
Fax: 615–741–3309

Texas
Department on Aging
4900 North Lamar, 4th floor
Austin, TX 78751
512–424–6840
Fax: 512–424–6890

Utah
Division of Aging and Adult Services
Dept. of Social Services
Box 45500
120 North, 200 West
Salt Lake City, UT 84145–0500
801–538–3910
Fax: 801–538–4395

Vermont
Aging and Disabilities
103 South Main St.
Waterbury, VT 05676
802–241–2400
Fax: 802–241–2325

Virginia
Dept. for the Aging
1600 Forest Ave.
Preston Bldg., Suite 102
Richmond, VA 23229
804–662–9333
Fax: 804–662–9354

Virgin Islands
Senior Citizens Affairs
Dept. of Human Services
#19 Estate Diamond Fredericksted
St. Croix, VI 00840
809–692–5950
Fax: 809–692–2062

Washington
Aging and Adult Services Administration
Dept. of Social and Health Services
P.O. Box 45050
Olympia, WA 98504–5050
360–586–8753
Fax: 360–902–7848

West Virginia
Bureau of Senior Services
1900 Kanawha Blvd., East
Holly Grove, Bldg. 10
Charleston, WV 25305–0160
304–558–3317
Fax: 304–558–0004

Wisconsin
Bureau of Aging and Long Term Care
    Resources
Dept. of Health and Family Services
217 S. Hamilton St., Suite 300
Madison, WI 53707
608–266–2536
Fax: 608–267–3203

Wyoming
Office on Aging
139 Hathaway Bldg.
Cheyenne, WY 82002–0710
307–777–7986
Fax: 307–777–5340

Eldercare Survey Tool

Part I

1. On a continuing basis, are you providing care (e.g. financial, housing, feeding, bathing, transportation, etc.) for a person over the age of 60?

Circle ONE   a. Yes - If Yes, please skip to Part II, Question 4.
letter   b. No - If No, please continue to Question 2.

2. Within the past five years, have you provided care (e.g. financial, housing, feeding, bathing, transportation, etc.) for a person over the age of 60?

Circle ONE   a. Yes - If Yes, please skip to Part II, Question 5.
letter   b. No - If No, please continue to Question 3.

3. Do you anticipate that in the next five years you will have to provide care (e.g. financial, housing, feeding, bathing, transportation, etc.) for a person over the age of 60?

Circle ONE   a. Yes - If Yes, please skip to Part III, Question 23.
letter   b. No - If No, please skip to Part IV, Question 24.

Part II: Information on Specific Care Provided

4. **Currently,** for how many persons over age 60 are you providing care?

_____ Persons

5. In the **past five years,** for how many persons over age 60 did you provide care - but are no longer?

_____ Persons

For the following questions, please provide separate answers for the one or two **main persons** over age 60 that you **currently** care for. If you **are not currently** caring for someone, skip to Part IV, Question 23.

Question	Person One	Person Two

6. What is your relationship to the person(s) for whom you care?
 	
Circle ONE letter
	a. Mother/Father
	b. Wife/Husband
	c. Grandmother/Grandfather
	d. Sister/Brother
	e. Mother-in-law/
	   Father-in-law
	f. Aunt/Uncle
	g. Stepmother/
	   Stepfather
	h. Other:
	
	_____
	(specify)
		a. Mother/Father
		b. Wife/Husband
		c. Grandmother/Grandfather
		d. Sister/Brother
		e. Mother-in-law/
		   Father-in-law
		f. Aunt/Uncle
		g. Stepmother/
		   Stepfather
		h. Other:
		
		_____
		(specify)

7. What is the gender of the person for whom you care?	a. Female b. Male	a. Female b. Male
8. What is the age of the person for whom you care?	_____ Years	_____ Years

9. For each person, what kind of care are you providing that they cannot do themselves?	a. Personal care
	   (cooking, bathing, etc.)
	b. Home maintenance
	c. Housekeeping
	d. Transportation
	   (to doctors, shopping, etc.)
		a. Personal care
		   (cooking, bathing, etc.)
		b. Home maintenance
		c. Housekeeping
		d. Transportation
		   (to doctors, shopping, etc.)

Question	Person One	Person Two
Circle all letters that apply.	e. Assistance with bill-paying (Medicare, insurance forms) f. General (dealing with homemaker, attorney, health care provider) g. Other: _____ (specify)	e. Assistance with bill-paying (Medicare, insurance forms) f. General (dealing with homemaker, attorney, health care provider) g. Other: _____ (specify)
10. Where does this person live? Circle ONE letter only	a. In your home b. Elsewhere locally c. Out of town	a. In your home b. Elsewhere locally c. Out of town
11. How long have you been providing this care?	a. Less than 6 months b. 6 months, but less than 2 years c. 2-5 years d. More than 5 years	a. Less than 6 months b. 6 months, but less than 2 years c. 2-5 years d. More than 5 years
12. Which of the following services does the person(s) receive from an outside individual, firm, or agency? Circle ALL that apply.	a. Homemaking chores (cleaning, etc.) b. Repairs and home maintenance c. Personal care d. Nursing services e. Home delivered meals f. Counseling g. Adult Day Care h. Transportation i. Other: _____ (specify)	a. Homemaking chores (cleaning, etc.) b. Repairs and home maintenance c. Personal care d. Nursing services e. Home delivered meals f. Counseling g. Adult Day Care h. Transportation i. Other: _____ (specify)

Part III: General Questions on Caregiving

In this section, we ask questions that relate to your caregiving responsibilities.

13. Have you had difficulty **finding suitable home care** services for your relative?	a. Yes b. No	a. Yes b. No
14. Have you had difficulty **affording care** or services ?	a. Yes b. No.	a. Yes b. No

Question	Person One	Person Two
15. Have you had difficulty **securing services** for your relative?	a. Yes b. No	a. Yes b. No

16. Who is the **primary** caregiver for your relative(s)?

a. Self	c. Other relative (e.g. brother sister)
b. Spouse	d. Non-relative

Circle ONE letter only.

17. On the **average**, how much time do you spend providing care for relatives over 60?

Circle ONE
letter only

a. Under 3 hours/week	d. 15-21 hours/week
b. 3-7 hours/week	e. Over 21 hours/week
c. 8-14 hours/week	

18. The yearly financial support that you provide as part of your caregiving amounts to:

Circle ONE
letter only

a. None	d. $2,500-$4,999/year
b. Under $1,000/year	e. $5,000/year or more
c. $1,000-$2,499/year	

19. Do you feel that your caregiving responsibilities interfere with your work life?

Circle ONE
letter only

a. Never	d. Frequently
b. Seldom	e. Very Frequently
c. Sometimes	

20. In an average month, how much time do you spend away from work (being absent or late) because of your caregiving responsibilities?

Circle ONE
letter only

a. None	d. 3-5 days
b. Less than a day	e. More than 5 days
c. 1-2 days	

21. From which of the following have you sought help at work for problems you are having in your caregiving role?

Circle ALL
that apply

a. Employee Assistance	d. Company health service
b. Personnel	e. Supervisor
c. Co-worker	f. No help sought from anyone in the work place.
	g. Other: _____
	(specify)

22. To date, where have you received most of your information about caregiving issues?

Circle ALL that apply	a. Government agency (such as the Area Agency on Aging)	e. Church, synagogue, or other religious institution
	b. Family/Friend	f. Media (newspaper, tv, radio)
	c. Internet	g. Employee Assistance Program
	d. Doctor, health care provider	h. Other: _____ (specify)

23. Please rate how helpful the following services would be in **your** caregiving situation.

Circle ONE number for each item. Rate all services.

Helpful	Not Helpful	Uncertain	
1	2	3	Flexible work hours and flexible leave
1	2	3	Before-tax deductions for dependent care
1	2	3	Extended leave of absence (3 months or more)
1	2	3	Adult day care services for frail elders who need some assistance during the day
1	2	3	Weekend, evening, or occasional relief from caregiving
1	2	3	Home care services, such as home health, personal care, homemaker
1	2	3	Chore services (for errands, home maintenance, housekeeping)
1	2	3	In-home health assessments to help in planning a course of action/care
1	2	3	Transportation available for elders from a residence to medical appointments, essential shopping
1	2	3	Assistance in finding and using adult residential services (e.g. nursing homes, homes for adults, group homes)
1	2	3	Workshops with information about Medicare/Medicaid, finances, community resources
1	2	3	Counseling

Question 23 (continued)
Please rate how helpful the following services would be in **your** caregiving situation.

Circle ONE number for each item. Rate all services.

Helpful	Not Helpful	Uncertain	
1	2	3	Support groups with other working caregivers that focus on helping you cope

Part IV: General Demographic Information

We are interested in developing a profile of all employees, whether or not they are caregivers. This information will help us to plan for future as well as current employee needs.

24. What is your age as of your last birthday? _____ Years

25. What is your gender?

Circle ONE letter   a. Female   b. Male

26. What is your ethnic background?

Circle ONE letter   a. White (non-Hispanic)   d. Hispanic
                     b. Black (non-Hispanic)   e. Other: _____
                     c. Asian/Pacific Islander

27. What is your marital status?

Circle ONE letter   a. Never married   d. Divorced
                     b. Married   e. Widowed
                     c. Separated

28. How many family members currently live in your household? (Please include all infants, children, and adults related to you by blood or marriage)

_____ People

29. What is the number of children under 18 who are dependent on you for financial or other care? (Do not include children who are financially independent)

_____ Children

30. What is the number of persons over age 18 and under 60 who are dependent on you for financial or other care?

_____ People

31. What is your annual Household Income? (Include all members of your household)

Circle ONE letter
a. Under $10,000
b. $10,000-29,999
c. $30,000-49,999
d. $50,000-74,999
e. $75,000-99,999
f. Above $100,000

32. How many years have you been employed by this company? _____ Years

33. How would you best describe your current type of job?

Circle ONE letter
a. Executive
b. Professional
c. Technical
d. Clerical
e. Paraprofessional
f. Skilled labor
g. Unskilled labor
h. Other: _____
(specify)

34. Are you employed:

Circle ONE letter   a. Full-time   b. Part-time

35. What do you feel are the main concerns and issues relating to the care of the elderly person? How can the following help?

a. Community:

_____
_____
_____
_____
_____
_____

b. Workplace:

_____
_____
_____
_____
_____
_____

Thank you for taking part in the survey. If you would like to share additional information regarding your caregiving responsibilities, please complete the following:
(Your response will be kept confidential)

Name: _____

Address: _____(Street) _____(City, State) _____(Zip)

Telephone: (____)_____(home) (____) _____(business)

Appendix C

Organizational Resources

The good news for managers involved in the development of elder care responses in the work place is that there are many reliable sources of information and technical advice. The bad news is that there are so many reliable sources of information and technical advice. If a manager chooses to enter into a contract with a local or national vendor of elder care resource and referral (R&R) services, the vendor will likely have a good grasp of all the aging-related resources needed. Without the assistance of an R&R vendor, managers can successfully network their way to finding the information needed by establishing a good working relationship with the staff of the State Unit on Aging (SUA) and the Area Agency on Aging (AAA) serving the community in which the employer's headquarters office is located. These two types of organizations, described under the Older Americans Act program, serve as central information repositories regarding the full spectrum of national, state, and local resources for the care of older persons.

This appendix includes an overview of the four key federal programs affecting older people and the families caring for them: the Social Security Act, the Older Americans Act, Medicare, and Medicaid. There are literally hundreds of other federal and state programs administered by dozens of federal and state agencies. However, for the purposes of program planning and implementation, the manager can access information about any specific program by contacting officials connected to one of these four major programs.

The remaining resources listed in this chapter are organized under two headings: Resources for Managers and Resources for Caregivers. The categories are not mutually exclusive. Many of the resources listed under the caregivers' category will also be of interest to managers and vice versa.

FOUR MAJOR FEDERAL PROGRAMS

Social Security Act

This federal legislation was passed in 1935 and created the Old Age Survivors and Disability Insurance Program, commonly referred to as Social Security. Disability insurance was added in 1956. The Social Security Act and various amendments are responsible for a substantial part of the federal safety net, including Medicare, Medicaid, the Supplemental Security Income (SSI) program, unemployment insurance, public health services, maternal and child health services, and social services block grants.

Title II of the act authorizes a social insurance program funded through employee and employer payroll taxes. Title XVI authorizes the SSI program for the aged, blind, and disabled. Titles XVIII and XIX authorize the Medicare and Medicaid programs, respectively.

There are three types of Social Security retirement, disability and survivorship benefits under Title II of the act:

- retirement benefits and disability benefits paid to insured workers
- benefits to dependents of retired or disabled workers
- survivorship benefits to the surviving family of a deceased worker, including a lump-sum death benefit payable to the deceased worker's family

Retirement, disability, and dependents' benefits are based on the insured worker's primary insurance amount and are subject to early retirement deductions or delayed retirement credits.

Like the Social Security program itself, the SSI program is administered by the Social Security Administration. Unlike Social Security, SSI is a means-tested program. The purpose of the program is to provide benefits based on need to individuals who are aged, blind, or disabled. The comprehensive SSI program replaced previously existing federally supported welfare programs for such individuals. In order to be eligible for SSI, a person must be either sixty-five or older, blind, or disabled, and may not have countable income or resources above specified levels. In 1996, federal legislation was enacted that gives states the option to exclude certain categories of legal aliens from receiving SSI benefits.

Older Americans Act

The Older Americans Act of 1965 (OAA), as amended, created the primary vehicle for organizing, coordinating and providing community-based services and opportunities for older Americans and their families. All individuals sixty years of age and older are eligible for services under the OAA, although priority attention is given those who are in greatest need. In FY 1997, the OAA appropriation was approximately $830 million for programs administered by the Administration on Aging (AoA), an agency of the U.S. Department of Health and Human Services that serves as the focal point and advocacy agency for older persons.

The National Aging Network

AoA provides leadership, technical assistance and support to the national aging network, which includes fifty-seven State Units on Aging, more than 660 Area Agencies on Aging, 222 tribal organizations representing 300 tribes, and thousands of service providers, senior centers, caregivers, and volunteers. Working in close partnership, the members of the aging network plan, coordinate and develop community-level systems of services designed to meet the needs of older persons and their caregivers.

State Units on Aging (SUAs)

AoA awards funds for home and community-based services to the SUAs, which are located in every state and U.S. territory. SUAs also receive funds for critical nutrition and support services, and elder rights programs including the nursing home ombudsman program, legal services, outreach and elder abuse prevention efforts. Appendix I lists the name, address and phone number of each of the SUAs.

Area Agencies on Aging (AAAs)

AAAs receive funds from their SUAs to plan, develop, coordinate and arrange for services to assist the older persons who are in greatest need in each planning and service area. AAAs generally cover substate regions. As a whole, the AAAs contract with 27,000 public and private agencies and groups to provide home and community-based care services. To obtain the name, address and telephone number of the AAA serving a particular community, call the SUA in that state or the Eldercare Locator service (described under Resources for Caregivers) at 800–677–1116.

Medicare

Medicare was established by Congress in 1965 as Title VIII of the Social Security Act. It is a federal health insurance program wholly funded by the federal government with no state participation. Its coverage is divided into Part A and Part B. The former basically covers acute care in hospitals and limited post hospital care in a skilled nursing facility and at home. Part B is a voluntary supplemental medical insurance for a variety of outpatient hospital services.

The Health Care Financing Administration (HCFA), a division of the U.S. Department of Health and Human Services, administers the Medicare program. Its day-to-day administration is operated through insurance provider companies. In the case of Part A, the insurance companies are called fiscal intermediaries, and in the case of Part B, they are called carriers. A medical review organization known as the peer review organization (PRO), as a private contractor for Medicare, participates to a limited extent in the administration of the Medicare program with responsibility for medical determinations in hospitals including matters relating to patient admissions and duration of stay. PROs also determine whether Medicare coverage is reasonable and necessary.

Six groups of persons are eligible for Medicare Part A benefits. The largest group is individuals age sixty-five or over entitled to Social Security retirement benefits. Also eligible are individuals receiving disability benefits for at least twenty-four months, individuals with end-stage renal disease, federal and state government employees, and transitional and voluntary enrollees.

Medicare Part B is a voluntary program for eligible individuals who enroll in the program and pay a premium quarterly or by having it deducted from their monthly Social Security checks. Eligibility for Part B does not depend on Part A eligibility, although all individuals over age sixty-five eligible for Part A are automatically eligible for Part B.

Medicaid

Medicaid (Title XIX of the Social Security Act) is a welfare program of medical assistance. Financed jointly by the state and federal governments, the program is administered primarily by the states. Individuals age sixty-five years of age and older, blind or disabled persons, low-income pregnant women, and certain low-income families with children may qualify for this assistance. Medicaid recipients must be American citizens or fall within specific categories of permanent resident aliens. According to the Personal Responsibility and Work Opportunity Reconciliation Act of 1996, states are now given some discretion to exclude certain resident aliens from receiving most services covered by the program.

Medicaid is a means-tested program. Unlike Medicare which is available regardless of financial need to most persons sixty-five or older and to certain disabled individuals, Medicaid is available only to individuals with limited income and assets. All the states participate in the Medicaid program.

Federal law requires that all states provide the categorically needy and the optional categorically needy recipient at least the following services: inpatient hospital services, outpatient hospital services, laboratory and X-ray services, nursing facility services for people over age twenty-one, early and periodic screening, diagnosis and treatment of people under age twenty-one, family planning services and supplies for individuals of childbearing age, physicians' services and some dental services, midwife services, home health care for those eligible for nursing facility services, and psychiatric care on an inpatient and outpatient basis.

Medicaid is the nation's largest funding source for long-term care. Of the foregoing services, nursing facility services and home health care services are most commonly associated with Medicaid long-term care. Nursing facility services are provided in institutional settings to individuals requiring skilled nursing or rehabilitative care or other health-related services above the level of room and board. Medicaid administers a waiver process that allows states to apply to HCFA for permission to provide home care to persons who would otherwise be institutionalized. Home care services provided under waivers include home delivered meals, home maintenance tasks, and respite care. In addition, specified personal care services may be provided through a personal care option granted to the states.

RESOURCES FOR MANAGERS

This section contains lists of recommended resources and readings, as well as organizations that can be of help in program design and implementation. There are many excellent books and reports on such topics as caring for older relatives, aging, and health. The publications listed here are those most useful for managers involved with elder care in the context of work/life program development.

Consulting Firms and Resource and Referral Vendors

The manager seeking advice and assistance with development of an elder care work place initiative can turn to a number of different sources, depending on the need. For profit and nonprofit firms provide consulting help, educational materials, and seminars, and offer resource and referral services.

Three national work/life firms have developed significant expertise in the delivery of quality elder care resource and referral services. Each of these firms provides elder care and child care resource and referral services for a client base that exceeds 1 million employees.

DCC/The Dependent Care Connection, Inc.

P.O. Box 2783

Westport, CT 06880

Telephone 203–226–2680

Fax 203–226–2853

Internet dccwebmaster@dcclifecare.com

Founded in 1984, DCC offers counseling, education and referral services that can accommodate the diverse needs of employee populations. In addition to offering a central elder care R&R service, DCC operates LifeCare Net, which delivers its R&R services over the World Wide Web and to employees connected to a corporate intranet.

Ceridian Performance Partners
8100 34th Ave. South
Minneapolis, MN 55425–1640
Telephone 800–788–1949
Fax 612–853–5270
Internet ceridian.performance.partners@ceridian.com

This firm is a leading Employee Assistance Program provider and now offers a spectrum of services for the full range of work/life issues, including a national elder care resource and referral service formerly administered by The Partnership Group.

WFD (formerly Work/Family Directions)
930 Commonwealth Ave.
Boston, MA 02215–1212
Telephone 617–278–4000
Fax 617–739–6794
Internet www.wfd.com

WFD, the largest vendor of child care and elder care services, is a consulting firm specializing in work force commitment and a leading provider of corporate work/life services. Under contract with IBM, Work/Family Directions established the first national elder care resource and referral service in 1988.

• • •

In addition to the three national firms listed, there are many local and regional organizations, both for profit and nonprofit, which provide the employer market dependent care and work/life balance services, including elder care consultation and referral and geriatric care management services. To locate these, refer to the local telephone yellow pages listings under such headings as "Work/Life Services," "Dependent Care Services," "Aging Services," and "Consulting Firms, Work/Family Benefits." The major national publications specializing in personnel and employee benefits issues regularly include listings of vendors of this kind.

Organizational Resources for Managers

Administration on Aging
U.S. Department of Health and Human Services
Washington, DC 20201
Phone 202–619–0724
Fax 202–401–7741
Internet www.aoa.dhhs.gov

The federal focal point for programs and services for older persons. See the Older Americans Act description previously mentioned for more information.

Alliance of Work/Life Professionals
465 Carlisle Drive
Herndon, VA 20170
Telephone 800–874–9383

Professional society dedicated to furthering the field through education and professional development activities.

American Society on Aging
833 Market Street
San Francisco, CA 94103
Telephone 800–537–9728
Fax 415–974–9600

ASA is a leading provider of professional education on aging in the United States. The mission of ASA is to promote the well-being of aging people and their families by enhancing the abilities and commitment of those who work with them. The ASA's Business Forum on Aging provides research, education, and networking opportunities for businesses that offer products and services to the older adult market. *Generations* is published quarterly and *Aging Today* is published bimonthly for members and subscribers.

Catalyst
250 Park Ave.
New York, NY 10003
Telephone 212–777–8900
Fax 212–477–4252

A private, nonprofit research organization which pursues the objective of enabling women in business and the professions to achieve their maximum potential and to help employers capitalize on the talents of their female employees.

The Conference Board, Inc.
845 Third Ave.
New York, NY 10022–6679
Telephone 212–759–0900
Fax 212–980–7014
Internet info@conference-board.org

Founded in 1916, the Conference Board's twofold purpose is to improve the business enterprise system and to enhance the contribution of business to society. To accomplish this, the Conference Board strives to be the leading global business membership organization that enables senior executives from all industries to explore and exchange ideas of impact on business policy and practices. The organization offers educational programs, conducts research, and publishes reports.

Families and Work Institute
330 Seventh Avenue
New York, NY 10001
Telephone 212–465–2044
Fax 212–465–8637

A nonprofit research and planning organization that conducts research on business, government, and community efforts to help employees balance their job and family responsibilities. The Institute offers a free catalog listing its publications.

The Gerontological Society of America
1275 K Street, N.W., Suite 350
Washington, DC 20005–4006
Telephone 202–842–1275
Fax 202–842–1150
Internet www.geron.org

The GSA is a professional organization that promotes the scientific study of aging in the biological and social sciences. GSA has conducted its annual scientific meeting since 1957. Publications include *The Gerontologist* and *The Journal of Gerontology*.

International Society for Work Time Options
c/o New Ways to Work
785 Market Street
San Francisco, CA 94103
Telephone 415–995–9860
Fax 415–995–9867

Society membership includes individuals and organizations working in the area of voluntary and flexible work options.

National Council on the Aging, Inc. (NCOA)
409 Third Street, S.W., Suite 200

Washington, DC 20024
Telephone 202–479–1200
Fax 202–479–0735
Internet www.ncoa.org

NCOA is a national, nonprofit organization that serves as a center of leadership, innovation, and nationwide expertise in the issues of aging. Membership includes individuals and organizations, professionals and volunteers, service providers, consumer and labor groups, businesses, government agencies, religious groups, and voluntary organizations. NCOA seeks to promote the well-being and contributions of older people and to enhance the field of aging. NCOA's quarterly magazine offers cross-cutting issues and emerging practice models. Other publications on topics of interest to older Americans are available on request.

National Institute on Aging (NIA)
Public Information Office
Building 31, Room 5C27
31 Center Drive MSC 2292
Telephone 301–496–1752
Fax 301–496–1072
Internet niainfo@access.digex.net

The NIA, part of the National Institutes of Health, is the federal government's principal agency for conducting and supporting biomedical, social, and behavioral research related to aging processes and the diseases and special problems of older people. The NIA operates an information clearinghouse resource at 800–222–2225.

Society for Human Resources Management
1800 Duke Street
Alexandria, VA 22314
Telephone 703–548–3440

A leading society of human resource management professionals offering excellent publications, educational programs, technical advice, and many other benefits.

ORGANIZATIONAL RESOURCES FOR CAREGIVERS

In addition to the organizations listed under Resources for Managers, the following are among the leading sources of information and support for working caregivers in the United States.

Alzheimers Disease and Related Disorders Association, Inc.
919 Michigan Ave., Suite 1000
Chicago, IL 60611–1676
Telephone 800–272–3900

The Alzheimers Association is a nonprofit membership organization which includes individuals and organizations. With two hundred chapters throughout the United States, the Association offers a wide variety of education, information, and support services for victims of Alzheimers disease and their family members including local referrals for assistance, respite care, and caregiver support groups. The Association offers many publications and educational materials, some free of charge.

American Association of Homes and Services for the Aging (AAHSA)
901 E Street, N.W., Suite 500
Washington, DC 20004–2037
Telephone 202–783–2242

AAHSA represents nonprofit housing providers and offers free brochures on housing options, skilled nursing facilities, and a guide to long-term care. A publications catalog is available upon request.

American Association of Retired Persons (AARP)
601 E Street, N.W.
Washington, DC 20049
Telephone 202–434–2277
Internet www.aarp.org

The largest membership organization of its kind, AARP offers free publications including *Caregivers Resource Kit* (free of charge, fulfillment #EE0926), and the *National Continuing Care Directory* by Anne Trueblood Raper, available for a fee (member discount). AARP maintains a national network of local chapters and provides information for caregivers and other aging topics on its website.

American Bar Association
Order Fulfillment Department
750 North Lake Shore Drive
Chicago, IL 60611
Telephone 800–621–6159

The ABA publishes *Planning for Life and Death* (order #PC: 543-0040-01) and *Wills: Why You Should Have One* (order #PC: 543-0039-01). Single copies provided free of charge.

American Self-Help Clearinghouse
St. Claire's Riverside Medical Center
25 Pocono Road
Denville, NJ 07834
Telephone 201–625–7101

The clearinghouse provides referrals to local support groups around the country affiliated with a particular disease.

Assisted Living Federation of America (ALFA)
9401 Lee Highway, Suite 402
Fairfax, VA 22031
Telephone 703–691–8100

ALFA provides professional education for its members and represents assisted living residences in legislative matters. ALFA includes affiliates in many states and offers a free consumer checklist for evaluating assisted living residences.

Children of Aging Parents (CAP)
Woodbourne Office Campus
1609 Woodbourne Road, Suite 302 A
Levittown, PA 19057
Telephone 215–945–6900

CAP operates a national clearinghouse on caregiver issues, resources, publications, local referrals to support groups and care managers, and it publishes *Capsule*, a monthly newsletter.

Choice In Dying
200 Varick Street, 10th floor
New York, NY 10014–0148
Telephone 800–989–WILL or 212–366–5540

Choice in Dying offers free publication of state-specific Living Will and Power of Attorney forms.

Eldercare Locator
Telephone 800–677–1116

This free service, funded by the federal Administration on Aging, can link consumers to specific elder care services anywhere in the United States.

Family Caregiver Alliance
425 Bush Street, Suite 500
San Francisco, CA 94018
Telephone 800–445–8106

The Alliance operates a clearinghouse for memory loss and brain injury. Extensive literature is available, as well as a publications list and services. The Alliance publishes the *Directory of California Support Groups for Caregivers of Brain Impaired Adults.*

Foundation for Hospice and Home Care
519 C Street, N.E.
Washington, DC 20002–5809
Telephone 202–547–6586

The Foundation publishes an extensive catalog of educational and training materials for consumers and caregivers and offers free caregiver guides, including *All About Hospice.*

Health Care Financing Administration
U.S. Department of Health and Human Services
200 Independence Ave., S.W.
Washington, DC 20201
Telephone 800–772–1213; Medicare Hotline: 800–638–6833

HCFA offers many free publications, including *Medicare Handbook, Guide to Health Insurance for People with Medicare*, and *Medicare and Advance Directives.* HCFA issues a quarterly list of all its publications.

Health Insurance Association of America
Consumer Information Service
555 13th Street, N.W., Suite 600 East
Washington, DC 20004–1109

This insurance trade association offers a free *Guide to Long Term Care Insurance* and publishes a list of companies offering long-term care insurance policies, available at no charge.

Health Insurance Counseling and Advocacy Program (HICAP)

A program that helps consumers understand their health insurance policies and make good choices among alternative health insurance programs. To find the HICAP serving a locality, call the State Unit on Aging or the State Insurance Commission, Division of Consumer Affairs.

Institute of Certified Financial Planners
3801 E. Florida Ave., Suite 708
Denver, CO 80210
Telephone 800–282–7526; 303–751–7600

The Institute will provide consumers a free list of Certified Financial Planners serving any locality in the United States. In addition, the Institute publishes a free brochure *Selecting a Qualified Financial Planning Professional: Twelve Questions to Consider.*

National Academy of Elder Law Attorneys
1604 North Country Club Road
Tucson, AZ 85716
Telephone 520–881–4005

The Academy will provide a list of local referrals for a fee and also offers a free booklet entitled *Questions and Answers When Looking for An Elder Law Attorney.*

National Adult Day Services Association (NADSA)
c/o The National Council on the Aging
409 3rd Street, S.W., Second Floor
Washington, DC 20024
Telephone 202–479–1200

NADSA will provide the following information free of charge: *Adult Day Care Fact Sheet, Why Adult Day Care?*, and *Your Guide to Selecting an Adult Day Center.*

National Association of Professional Geriatric Care Managers
1604 North Country Club Road
Tucson, AZ 85716
Telephone 520–881–8008

This professional association will provide information and referrals to care managers throughout the United States. The association will send a listing of care managers in a local area upon receipt of a stamped, self-addressed envelope.

National Association of Insurance Commissioners (NAIC)
120 West 12th Street, Suite 1100
Kansas City, MO 64105
Telephone 816–842–3600

NAIC will send consumers a free brochure entitled *A Shopper's Guide to Long Term Care Insurance.*

National Center on Elder Abuse
810 First Street, N.E., Suite 500
Washington, DC 20036–2211
Telephone 212–682–2470

The Center offers a free information packet that includes articles, statistics, and a publications catalog. The Center can also provide referrals to state protective service agencies.

National Association for Home Care (NAHC)
228 7th Street, S.E.
Washington, DC 20003
Telephone 202–547–7424
Fax 202–547–5277
Internet www.nahc.org

NAHC, a professional organization, represents a variety of agencies providing home care services, including home health agencies, hospice programs, and home-maker home health aide agencies. NAHC develops professional standards for home care agencies, offers continuing education programs, monitors federal legislation, and provides information to consumers about selecting a home care provider. Publishes monthly *Caring* magazine and other publications for members.

National Caucus and Center on Black Aged, Inc. (NCCBA)
1424 K Street, N.W., Suite 500
Washington, DC 20005
Telephone 202–637–8400

The NCCBA is a nonprofit organization that works to improve the quality of life for older black Americans. The *COBAS Newsletter* and *Golden Age* are published quarterly.

National Citizens Coalition for Nursing Home Reform
1424 16th Street, N.W., Suite 202
Washington, DC 20036–2211
Telephone 202–332–2275

In addition to its legislative and regulatory "watchdog" role, this consumer advocacy organization connects individuals to local aging resources and publishes a catalog listing consumer guides for sale.

National Council of Senior Citizens (NCSC)
1331 F Street, N.W., Suite 800
Washington, DC 20004–1171
Telephone 202–624–9340

NCSC's Nursing Home Information Center includes a nursing home locator service. NCSC also publishes a nursing home residents' *Bill of Rights* and a *Coping with Aging* series.

National Family Caregivers Association
9621 East Bexhill Drive
Kensington, MD 20895–3104
Telephone 800–896–3650
Fax 301–942–2302
Internet www.nfcacares.org

NFCA is a nonprofit membership organization dedicated to making life better for all of America's family caregivers. Services to members include education, information, support and validation, public awareness, and advocacy. NFCA strive to minimize the disparity between a caregiver's quality of life and that of mainstream America. Benefits include *Take Care!* newsletter, the caregiver-to-caregiver peer support network, *The Resourceful Caregiver* resource guide, and *Cards for Caregivers*, a program that sends a different, upbeat message three times a year to remind caregivers that they are not alone. NFCA operates a speakers bureau and public awareness campaign.

National Hispanic Council on Aging
2713 Ontario Road, N.W., Suite 200
Washington, DC 20013–1133
Telephone 202–265–1288

The Council provides information and advocacy, including a newsletter, brochures, and a number of books available for sale.

National Hospice Organization (NHO)
1901 North Moore Street, Suite 901
Arlington, VA 22209
Telephone 800–658–8898

NHO provides information, literature and other resources for consumers and represents its members in legislative and regulatory affairs.

National Indian Council on Aging
6400 Uptown Blvd., N.E.
City Center, Suite 510W
Albuquerque, NM 87110
Telephone 505–888–3302

The council provides information and referrals for Indians and Alaskan natives nationwide.

Older Women's League (OWL)
666 11th Street, N.W., Suite 700
Washington, DC 20001
Telephone 202–783–6686

OWL publishes reports and other materials on topics including older women and poverty, caregiving, pensions, legal, housing, and long-term care.

Shepard's Centers of America
6700 Troost, Suite 616
Kansas City, MO 64131
Telephone 816–523–1080

The Shepard's Centers are interfaith ministry programs that include home services such as hospice, handyman, shopping, transportation, respite care, meals, and telephone reassurance.

Social Security Administration (SSA)
6401 Security Blvd., Room 4J5
West High Rise, Baltimore, MD 21235
Telephone 800–772–1213

The SSA provides many free publications, such as *Understanding Social Security, Medicare and Coordinated Care Plans*, and *Hospice Benefits*. Telephone counselors answer questions and set up appointments as needed.

United Seniors Health Cooperative (USHC)
1331 H Street, N.W., Suite 500
Washington, DC 20005–4706
Telephone 202–393–6222

USHC benefits counselors make use of a computerized database to help consumers determine their eligibility for public programs and other forms of assistance. USHC will send a catalog of its many publications, and its counselors will provide referrals to similar services throughout the country.

Appendix D

Abbreviations and Acronyms

Like most professional disciplines, the field of aging and elder care has its own language and terminology. This appendix includes an alphabetical listing of abbreviations and acronyms used in elder care, accompanied by definitions of these commonly used terms.[1]

AAA (Area Agency on Aging). Under the Older Americans Act (OAA), the federal government distributes funds for various aging programs through State Units on Aging (SUA) which, in turn, fund local AAAs ("triple As"). These funds are used by local AAAs to support a wide variety of programs that assist older people.

AAPCC (Adjusted Annual Per Capita Cost). The basis of payment for Medicare-risk HMOs, the AAPCC is a yearly projection of program spending in Medicare's fee-for-service program. Medicare pays HMOs 95 percent of the AAPCC for each enrolled Medicare beneficiary, with adjustments for such factors as geographic cost differences (by county), age, sex, and disability status.

ADL (Activity of Daily Living). See also Instrumental Activities of Daily Living (IADL). Activities usually performed for oneself in the course of a normal day. Although definitions differ, ADLs are usually considered to be mobility (e.g., transfer from bed to chair), dressing, bathing, self-feeding, and toileting.

AIME (Average Indexed Monthly Earnings). The average indexed monthly earnings of a worker adjusted for inflation are used to calculate Social Security benefits. The AIME is determined by dividing total indexed earnings (the years of highest earnings up to the countable years) by the number of countable years, converted to months. Countable years used to determine the AIME of workers born after 1928 are the highest thirty-five years of earnings, whereas the AIME of older or deceased workers is based on record (i.e., actual) years.

ALJ (Administrative Law Judge). The appeals structure of the Social Security Administration (SSA) involves appeals related to Social Security, Supplemental Security Income (SSI) claims, and Medicare claims from decisions at the initial determination and reconsideration levels. Appeals from these decisions are brought before an ALJ at a hearing. ALJs have special training to review the lower level determinations and have the authority to accept or review decisions.

AoA (Administration on Aging [U.S.]). See also Older Americans Act. The Federal agency under the Department of Health and Human Services that administers the Older Americans Act.

CCRC (Continuing Care Retirement Community). This type of housing alternative, sometimes called a life care community, generally requires that an individual be able to live independently upon becoming a resident of the community. As a resident begins to need more assistance, specific additional services are made available. Most CCRCs offer three basic levels of housing on an as-needed basis: fully independent living, assisted living (personal care services), and skilled nursing care. Generally, a CCRC will charge an entrance fee as well as a monthly payment for its services.

CHHA (Certified Home Health Agency). A public or private organization that specializes in providing skilled nursing services, therapeutic services such as physical therapy, and home health aide services. A patient must receive these from a certified home health agency in order for Medicare or Medicaid to cover payment for them. To be certified, a home health agency must meet certain Medicaid and Medicare conditions of participation before it can receive payment from these programs. Among other conditions, certification requires an agency's compliance with patients' rights and with state and federal law.

COBRA (Consolidated Omnibus Reconciliation Act of 1985). This federal legislation requires that an employer must continue to provide medical insurance for a specified time for an employee, after the employee has left his or her employment. This so-called COBRA coverage is for the medical insurance that the employer then has in effect and is at the employee's sole expense.

COLA (Cost-of-Living Adjustment). Usually referred to as COLA, Social Security and SSI benefits received in January are increased annually by the increase in inflation. The COLA is based on changes in the consumer price index.

CSRA (Community Spouse's Resource Allowance). Also called a minimum monthly needs allowance, this term refers to the amount of income that states are required to permit an institutionalized individual, who is married and receiving Medicaid assistance, to contribute to his or her spouse remaining in the community in order to bring that spouse's income up to the minimum monthly allowance. Alternatively, states may also allow resources to be retained by the community spouse in sufficient amount to generate income to raise his or her income to the level of the minimum monthly needs allowance. It is the difference, if any, between the minimum monthly needs allowance and any income otherwise available to the spouse.

DME (Durable Medical Equipment). The rental or purchase of durable medical equipment for use in a patient's home is paid for under Medicare Part B, subject to a 20-percent coinsurance payment by the patient.

DNR (Do Not Resuscitate order). An order by an attending physician, patient consent (or possibly, by surrogate consent) that directs hospital personnel not to revive the patient if cardiopulmonary arrest occurs.

DRG (Diagnosis Related Group). This is a prospective payment system used by Medicare to reimburse acute care hospitals. Under this system, a standard flat rate per hospital admission is prospectively established by and paid for by Medicare regardless of the hospital's cost of providing that care. Patients' illnesses or injuries are classified according to a list of 490 DRGs. Each DRG is assigned a numerical value, such as a stated dollar amount for a stroke.

ECHO (Elder Cottage Housing Opportunity). Sometimes called a granny flat or an in-law apartment, this unit is a small, manufactured home that can be installed in the back or side of a single family residence and removed when it is no longer needed. It is specifically designed for older persons and persons with disabilities and is intended to enable them to live close to their family or younger friends who will provide the support necessary for them to live independently. The addition of an ECHO unit to an existing house or property is contingent upon local zoning regulations.

EOMB (Explanation of Medicare Benefits). A notice from the Medicare insurance carrier informing the patient how much it has paid for a service covered by Medicare Part B, the services covered and charges approved. For services for which a doctor or other provider has taken assignment, the carrier pays the doctor or other provider directly. For unassigned services, the carrier pays the patient, and he or she is responsible for paying the provider.

EPO (Exclusive Provider Organization). An EPO is a variant type of an HMO and provides an exclusive hospital and physician network from which a member must obtain health care services. A member who selects a hospital or physician from outside the network bears the entire cost of such services.

ERISA (Employee Retirement Income Security Act). This 1974 law provides Federal protection to and defines rights of employees under pension plans. A plan that meets ERISA requirements and is voluntarily provided by an employer is known as a qualified plan.

ESRD (End Stage Renal Disease). Kidney disease that is severe enough to require lifetime dialysis or a kidney transplant. ESRD patients are eligible for Medicare and may be eligible for Social Security payments if found to be disabled.

FHA (Farmers Home Administration). The Farmers Home Administration is a home financing agency within the U.S. Department of Agriculture. FHA programs are limited to jurisdictions with less than 20,000 residents. Some FHA multifamily rental developments are restricted to people who are at least sixty-two years of age or disabled.

HCFA (Health Care Financing Administration). This Federal agency is part of the U.S. Department of Health and Human Services and is responsible for Medicare and Medicaid administration and regulations. It also administers the programs under which HMOs can enroll persons eligible for Medicare.

HHS (U.S. Department of Health and Human Services).

HICAP (Health Insurance Counseling and Assistance Program). To help Medicare beneficiaries understand their health insurance coverage and options, HCFA grants states funds to set up and operate this volunteer-based counseling program. Its name varies from state to state. In most states, the Area Agencies on Aging are the local administrators of HICAPs whose mission is to provide unbiased information not only about standard Medicare insurance and Medicare HMOs but also about Medigap policies, Medicaid, and long-term care insurance options.

HIO (Health Insuring Organization). HIOs are Medicaid managed care organizations that pay for the services of subcontracting providers and assume all financial risk in exchange for a premium.

HMO (Health Maintenance Organization). HMOs are a form of managed care provided to participants (enrollees) under a medical benefits plan, featuring a network of doctors, hospitals, and other health care providers. An individual may enroll in an HMO on his or her own, or as a participant of a group plan offered by an employer or an association. HMOs undertake to provide all of the care necessary for a given beneficiary, acting in essence as an insurer as well as a provider. Thus, HMOs integrate insurance and health care delivery into one organization.

HUD (U.S. Department of Housing and Urban Development).

IADL (Instrumental Activity of Daily Living). See also Activities of Daily Living. These are activities ancillary to activities of daily living. The term includes light housework, preparing meals, shopping, using the telephone, keeping track of money or bills, and the taking of medicines. Services to assist with these activities are not covered by Medicare.

ICF (Intermediate Care Facility). A medical facility previously recognized under the Medicaid program and licensed under state law to provide, on a regular basis, health care services to residents who do not require the degree of care provided by a hospital or a skilled nursing facility (SNF), but who do require health services beyond just board and lodging that can be made available through an institutional facility.

IPA (Independent Practice Association). One of three models into which traditional HMOs are classified. In contrast to staff and group models, this model is an HMO with which an organization of physicians, or an IPA, contracts for only a portion of their practices. Physicians in the IPA provide care for the HMO's enrollees at a capitated rate or fee-for-service rate paid to the IPA, which in turn pays the participating physicians. The physicians work in their own settings.

IRA (Individual Retirement Account). This is an individual's private retirement account, created by the individual to accumulate resources to support his or her retirement years. The individual may annually contribute limited amounts of money to the IRA on a tax-deductible basis, which may be invested by the IRA and together with the income earned on the investments accumulate tax free. Income tax will be imposed upon the amounts in the IRA upon distribution.

LPN (Licensed Practical Nurse). A nurse who has completed a practical nursing program and is licensed by a state to provide routine patient care under the direction of a registered nurse or physician.

LTC (Long-Term Care). There is no single definition recognized for this term broadly covering the provision of services to people who are limited in their ability to function independently over a relatively long period of time. The long-term assistance provided to such persons consists of, among other things, help in performing basic activities of daily living and may also include services such as housework, laundry, grocery shopping, giving medication, and transportation. Long-term care also embraces skilled therapeutic care for the treatment and management of chronic conditions. Long-term care can be provided in home and community-based settings as well as in institutions such as nursing homes and assisted living facilities. The major sources of funding for long-term care are the private funds of older people and their families; government programs such as Medicaid and those authorized by the Older Americans Act; long-term care insurance; and assistance from not-for-profit local community agencies. Because Medicare is designed to cover acute care, its support of long-term care is limited.

LTCI (Long-Term Care Insurance). In order to help people protect against the high cost of long-term care either in a nursing home or at home, the insurance industry in the 1980s began to offer long-term care insurance. Since neither Medicare, Medicare supplemental insurance, nor private health insurance are intended to cover chronic conditions or long-term care, especially custodial care, LTCI policies were created to fill this gap. Federal legislation allows a portion of LTCI premiums to be tax deductible.

MSA (Medical Savings Account). The general concept of a medical savings account (MSA) is for an employer, or the government in the case of Medicare, to enable an insured individual to obtain and pay for a high deductible catastrophic health insurance policy. The employer or the government would pay a fixed premium to the catastrophic insurance company, and the insured individual would share the cost of the premium. The difference between what the employer or government would customarily pay for traditional coverage, and the premium of the catastrophic health insurance coverage would be put into an individual's MSA for his or her qualified medical expenses.

The Health Insurance Portability and Accountability Act of 1996 created a four-year experimental MSA program, effective January 1, 1997, allowing a maximum of 750,000 individuals in businesses with fifty or fewer employees as well as self-employed and uninsured individuals to receive favorable tax treatment for the MSA.

MSO (Management Services Organization). An MSO links one or more medical groups or physicians together with a hospital which is usually a wholly owned, for-profit subsidiary of a hospital/physician joint venture. Through utilization of an MSO, many individual physicians or small physician groups are able to access managed care plans.

NORC (Naturally Occurring Retirement Community). An apartment building, complex, or community, in which, due to the longevity of the residents and their aging in place, the majority of the residents are sixty years of age or older. In such situations, an informal support system may develop where residents look out for one another.

OAA (Older Americans Act). The Older Americans Act (OAA) was first passed in 1973 and subsequently has been amended during reauthorizations. The OAA created a three-tiered national aging network to administer the act, manage programs serving older people, and distribute federal funds. See Chapter 6 for a description of the elements and functions of each of the three tiers of the aging network: national, state, and local.

OASDI (Old-Age, Survivors, and Disability Insurance). This is the formal name for the Social Security Program, benefiting retirees, the disabled, and their families as authorized under Title II of the Social Security Act.

OBRA (Omnibus Budget Reconciliation Act). Passed almost every year since 1980, OBRA in one piece of legislation mandates changes in Federal programs in order to reconcile the budget to existing legislation. In the context of elder rights issues, OBRA '87 contains the Nursing Home Reform Law of 1987.

PACE (Program for All-Inclusive Care for the Elderly). This is a Medicare and Medicaid demonstration project, originally tested in ten sites, that targets frail elderly persons living at home who are eligible for nursing home care. The program integrates health and long-term care services in an adult day care setting and uses a multidisciplinary case management team of providers, including physicians, nurses, social workers, nutritionists, occupational and speech therapists, and health and transportation personnel. PACE providers are paid a fixed monthly fee. Medicare and Medicaid share the cost risk with the PACE site for a period of years, after which time the entire risk shifts to the PACE site.

PBGC (Pension Benefit Guarantee Corporation). A Federal agency that collects premiums from employers under an insurance scheme designed to guarantee payment of benefits under defined benefit pension plans, but not defined contribution plans.

PEBE (Personal Earnings and Benefits Estimate). Individual workers can request a personal earnings and benefits estimate from the Social Security Administration. This estimate shows Social Security-covered earnings and taxes paid for every year after 1950, the number of quarters needed for insured status, the number of quarters credited to the record, and various benefit estimates based on the information in the earnings record supplied by the worker.

PERS (Personal Emergency Response System). Equipment that monitors the safety of older people in their homes through signals electronically transmitted over the telephone to a twenty-four-hour emergency monitoring center. A PERS is a small device worn around the neck or wrist that allows the wearer to signal for help by pressing a button that activates the system. Consumers can purchase, rent, or lease this equipment.

PHO (Physician Hospital Organization). Basically, a PHO is formed when a hospital acquires or has a contractual relationship with a group of physicians. The hospital most commonly controls administrative matters, and physicians manage clinical aspects of the business. The PHO negotiates and manages capitation contracts for the physicians and hospitals.

PIA (Primary Insurance Amount). The PIA is the figure from which almost all Social Security cash benefit amounts are derived, including monthly benefits, their dependents, and their survivors. The PIA is based on a formula which takes various percentages of an individual's taxable earnings averaged over his or her working lifetime.

POS (Point of Service). A form of managed care offered by organizations such as HMOs. POS organizations feature a network of doctors, hospitals, and other health care providers. Participants have a choice of using the network or any other provider each time they seek medical care. This is a point of service choice.

PPO (Preferred Provider Organization). An arrangement between an employer or insurance company and a network of health care providers whereby the providers, called preferred providers, furnish health services in return for the guarantee of a certain volume of patients. As part of the arrangement, the employer or insurance company negotiates discounted fees with the PPO so that the insured enrollees receive services from the providers on a lower than customary fee-for-service basis.

PRO (Peer Review Organization). A PRO is a group of practicing doctors and other health care professionals who are paid by the Federal government to review the care given to Medicare patients. Part of the prospective payment system, PROs are under contract with the U.S. Department of Health and Human Services. Each state has a PRO.

QMB (Qualified Medicare Beneficiary). Federal law requires state Medicaid programs to "buy in" Medicare coverage for low-income Medicare beneficiaries generally unable to afford the required payments to obtain Medicare benefits. The buy-in consists of payment of deductibles and coinsurance costs under Medicare Part A and Part B, and payment of premiums under Part B, and, where necessary, under Part A. These beneficiaries are known as Qualified Medicare Beneficiaries. A subset of QMBs is known as dual-eligibles. They are eligible for and entitled to a full spectrum of both Medicare and Medicaid benefits. QMBs who are not dual eligibles are entitled only to the buy-in of their Medicare coverage.

RBRVS (Resource Based Relative Value Scale). An index that assigns weights to each medical service provided by physicians. The weights represent the relative amounts to be paid for each service. To fix the fee for a service, the index for that service is multiplied by a constant dollar amount, known as the conversion factor.

RN (Registered Nurse).

RUG (Resource Utilization Group). For Medicaid recipients, access to a nursing home is limited to those recipients of applicants who qualify medically for nursing facility care, according to an assessment procedure and criteria. The criteria are set forth in forms called a patient review instrument and a patient screening instrument, which are used to determine whether individuals need care in a nursing home or can be cared for in another setting such as their own home or other facility. Based on this assessment, a patient is assigned a resource utilization group (RUG), depending on the person's medical condition, care needs, and relative independence or dependence in performing activities of daily living. There are sixteen RUG categories, each indicating the amount a nursing facility will be reimbursed by Medicaid and the kind of care and staff time that will be needed.

SHMO (Social Health Maintenance Organization). An SHMO is a variant of classic HMOs and very limited in number. They are experimental demonstration projects funded by HCFA in ten states in which the project supplements Medicare benefits available through a TEFRA-risk HMO and in addition, provides prescription drugs plus homemaker services, respite care, medical transportation, adult day health care, and home health services. SHMO enrollees are locked in and may only receive Medicare coverage from that organization. Financing is through prepaid capitated funding jointly by Medicare and Medicaid (for Medicaid-eligible individuals) and through member premiums and copayments. HCFA tracks the results of these demonstrations in order to evaluate the model as a potentially cost-effective integrated method of financing and delivering long-term care.

SNF (Skilled Nursing Facility). Prior to 1990, Medicaid distinguished between a skilled nursing facility and intermediate nursing facility, with the former providing care primarily by or under the direct supervision of licensed nursing personnel. Since October 1990, Medicaid subsumed these two categories of facilities under the term "nursing facility."

TEFRA (Tax Equity and Fiscal Responsibility Act). A TEFRA risk contract is one of the two types of contracts that HCFA enters into with an HMO—known as a TEFRA risk HMO, or more simply as a risk HMO—so that it qualifies as a Medicare HMO. The TEFRA law established the rules governing these contracts.

URC (Utilization Review Committee). The URC is responsible for making decisions as to the medical necessity and reasonableness of care for extended stays in hospitals and skilled nursing facilities. An adverse finding by a URC will likely lead to a denial of Medicare coverage. However, a URC decision is not an initial determination subject to appeal.

NOTE

1. Source for the abbreviations, acronyms, and definitions of terms: Walter Feldesman, *Dictionary of Eldercare Terminology* (Washington, D.C.: United Seniors Health Cooperative, 1997), xv–xvii.

Annotated Bibliography

RECOMMENDED READINGS FOR MANAGERS

Campbell, Alice, and Marci Koblenz. *The Work and Life Pyramid of Needs: A New Paradigm for Understanding the Nature of Work and Life Conflicts*. Deerfield, Ill.: Baxter Healthcare and MK Consultants, 1997. This in-depth study of the work/life needs of employees of a major U.S. corporation is remarkable for its formulation of a rational approach to dealing with work/life balance needs. The authors suggest an action plan that simultaneously focuses on the sources of worker's greatest distress and sets priorities in a way that maximizes the employer's investment.

Doress-Worters, Paula B., and Diana Laskin Siegal. *The New Ourselves, Growing Older: Women Aging with Knowledge and Power*. New York: Simon & Schuster, 1994. An excellent source of frank and complete information on women's personal health in the second half of life.

Esty, Katharine, Richard Griffin, and Marcie Schorr Hirsch. *Workplace Diversity: A Manager's Guide to Solving Problems and Turning Diversity into a Competitive Advantage*. Holbrook, Mass.: Adams Media, 1995. An effective desktop reference that provides insight and practical guidance for solving everyday problems relating to the ten dimensions of diversity (including age, family situation, and physical ability or disability that relate to caregiving).

Feldesman, Walter. *Dictionary of Eldercare Terminology*. Washington, D.C.: United Seniors Health Cooperative, 1997. An essential reference for any professional working with or advising working caregivers. Includes definitions and program descriptions from "accelerated benefits" (under life insurance contracts) to "x-rays" (Medicare coverage of).

Galinsky, Ellen, James T. Bond, and Dana E. Friedman. *The Changing Workforce.* Edited by Brian Hackett. New York: Families and Work Institute, 1993. Summarizes key findings from an in-depth survey of a representative group of over 3,000 employees of leading corporations. Covers an extensive range of work/ life balance issues, including child care and elder care. Includes implications of the survey findings for policy and program planning.

Genovese, Rosalie G. *Americans at Mid-Life: Caught between Generations.* Westport, Conn.: Bergen & Garvey, 1997.

Hackett, Brian, ed. *The New Deal in Employment Relationships.* New York: The Conference Board, 1996. The Conference Board conducted a meeting of its Inter-Council group in March 1996, at which business executives from a variety of industries examined and challenged conventional views of the changing employee–employer relationship. This report provides new perspectives and challenges assumptions about how and why this relationship is changing.

Hayflick, Leonard. *How and Why We Age.* New York: Ballantine Books, 1994. A modern classic which entertainingly presents the facts and theories that shape our understanding of the social, biological, psychological, demographic, and economic dimensions of aging.

National Alliance for Caregiving (NAC) and American Association of Retired Persons (AARP), *Family Caregiving in the U.S.: Findings from a National Survey* (Washington, D.C.: NAC and AARP, 1997). The most comprehensive study undertaken to date, documenting the characteristics and needs of America's more than 22 million family caregivers.

National Institute on Aging (NIA) and Administration on Aging (AoA). *Resource Directory for Older People.* Bethesda, Md.: NIA Publications Office, 1996. An essential reference work listing over 240 federal and state agencies, private organizations, and associations concerned with the health care, social services, housing, employment, education, and nutrition needs of older persons. Each listing includes a statement of the organization's mission and services and publications provided, as well as street addresses, phone numbers, and Internet addresses. NIA publication #95-73B. To order a free copy, call (301) 496–1752.

The National Report on Work and Family. Silver Spring, Md.: Business Publishers, Inc. A biweekly newsletter providing news on legislation, litigation, and employer policies. Annual subscription fee. Internet address is: www.bpinews.com

Neal, Margaret B., Nancy J. Chapman, Berit Ingersoll-Dayton, and Arthur C. Emlen. *Balancing Work and Caregiving for Children, Adults, and Elders.* Newbury Park, Calif.: Sage Publications, 1993. Promotes an understanding of the commonalities and differences among those working caregivers caring for children, younger adults, and elders, as well as those who have multiple caregiving roles. Excellent summary of research and organizational responses.

Nouwen, J. M., and Walter J. Gaffney. *Aging: The Fulfillment of Life.* New York: Image Books, 1990. A rare, pithy work that challenges the reader to suspend traditionally held views and embrace aging as an opportunity to deepen one's understanding of life.

Olmsted, Barney, and Suzanne Smith. *Managing in a Flexible Workplace.* New York: AMACOM, 1997. Practical, easy-to-use guide to the full range of flexible work arrangements that can support work/life balance initiatives.

Riekse, Robert J., and Henry Holstege. *Growing Older In America*. New York: McGraw-Hill, 1996.
Wagner, Donna. *Caring Across the Miles—Findings of a Survey of Long Distance Caregivers*. Washington, D.C.: National Council on the Aging, 1997. The first national study that describes the characteristics and needs of long distance caregivers, and how they differ from caregivers in general.

VIDEO FOR MANAGERS

Growing Old in a New Age. South Burlington, Vt.: The Anneberg/CPB Collection, 1993. This video series features the emotional and physical processes of aging, stages of life, and the impact of aging on society. Toll-free number is (800)LEARNER.

A BASIC WORK PLACE LIBRARY
FOR FAMILY CAREGIVERS

Aging Parents: The Family Survival Guide. San Francisco, Calif.: Sybervision Systems, Inc., 1996. This combination of two videotapes plus an Action Guide workbook is a uniquely useful resource for family caregivers of aging parents. Endorsed by the National Council on the Aging and other leading aging groups, *Aging Parents* presents information in an easy-to-access, problem-solving format. It is an essential tool for family members. This guide can serve as the cornerstone for a work place resource library for family caregivers.
Caposella, Cappy, and Sheila Warnock. *Share the Care: How to Organize a Group for Someone Who is Seriously Ill*. New York: Fireside Books, 1995.
Carter, Rosalynn, and Susan K. Golant. *Helping Yourself Help Others: A Book for Caregivers*. New York: Times Books, 1994.
Cohen, Donna, and Carl Eisdorfer. *Caring for Your Aging Parents*. New York: G. P. Putnam's Sons, 1993.
Cole, Harry. *Helpmates: Support in Times of Critical Illness*. Louisville, Ky.: John Knox Press, 1991. Of special relevance for spousal caregivers.
Greenberg, Vivian. *Your Best Is Good Enough: Aging Parents and Your Emotions*. New York: Lexington Books, 1989.
Heath, Angela. *Long Distance Caregiving: A Survival Guide for Far Away Caregivers*. San Luis Obispo, Calif.: Impact Publishers, 1993.
Hirshfeld, Robert, and Susan Meltsner. *When the Blues Won't Go Away*. New York: Macmillan, 1991.
Horowitz, Karen E., and Douglas M. Lanes. *Witness to Illness: Strategies for Caregiving and Coping*. Reading, Mass.: Addison-Wesley, 1992.
Karr, Katherine L. *Taking Time for Me: How Caregivers Can Effectively Deal with Stress*. Buffalo, N.Y.: Prometheus Books, 1992.
Loverde, Joy. *The Complete Elder Care Planner: Where to Start, Questions to Ask and How to Find Help*. New York: Hyperion, 1997.
Lowe, Paula. *Carepooling*. San Francisco, Calif.: Berrett-Koehler, 1993.
Mace, Nancy, and Peter Rabbins. *The 36-Hour Day: A Family Guide to Caring for Persons with Alzheimer's Disease*. Baltimore, Md.: Johns Hopkins University Press, 1981.

Markham, Ursula. *Bereavement: Your Questions Answered*. Rockport, Mass.: Element Books, 1996.

Morris, Virginia. *How To Care for Aging Parents*. New York: Workman Publishing, 1996.

National Family Caregivers Association. *The Resourceful Caregiver: Helping Family Caregivers Help Themselves*. Hanover, Md.: Mosby Lifeline, 1996.

Pohl, Melvin, and J. Deniston. *Staying Sane When You Care for Someone with a Chronic Illness*. Deerfield Beach, Fla.: Health Communications, 1993.

Pollin, Irene. *Taking Charge: Overcoming the Challenges of Long Term Illness*. New York: Times Books, 1994.

Pritikin, Enid, and Trudy Reece. *Parentcare Survival Guide: Helping Your Folks Through the Not-So-Golden Years*. Hauppauge, N.Y.: Barron's, 1993.

Rando, Theresa A. *How to Go On Living When Someone You Love Dies*. Lexington, Mass.: D. C. Heath and Co., 1991.

Sherman, James R. *The Caregiver Survival Series*. Golden Valley, Minn.: Pathway Books, 1994–1995.

Strong, Maggie. *Mainstay*. Northampton, Mass.: Bradford Books, 1997. Of special relevance for spousal caregivers.

Index

ABOUT THE AUTHOR

John Paul Marosy is founder and President of Bringing Eldercare Home, a planning, training, and management consulting firm specializing in elder care, based in Worcester, Massachusetts. He is a former family caregiver and has served as CEO of leading organizations in the fields of aging and home health care.